LIFE AND DEATH IN THE TEMPLO MAYOR

Eduardo Matos Moctezuma

translated by

Bernard R. Ortiz de Montellano

Thelma Ortiz de Montellano

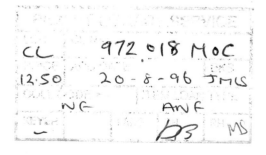

©1995 by the University Press of Colorado

Published by the University Press of Colorado
P. O. Box 849
Niwot, Colorado 80544

The University Press of Colorado is a cooperative publishing enterprise supported, in part, by Adams State College, Colorado State University, Fort Lewis College, Mesa State College, Metropolitan State College of Denver, University of Colorado, University of Northern Colorado, University of Southern Colorado, and Western State College of Colorado.

Library of Congress Cataloging-in-Publication Data

Moctezuma, Eduardo Matos
    [Vida y muerte en el Templo Mayor. English]
    Life and Death in the Templo Mayor / Eduardo Matos Moctezuma ;
translated by Bernard R. Ortiz de Montellano, Thelma Ortiz de
Montellano
        p. cm.
    Includes bibliographical references and index.
    ISBN 0-87081-400-1 (pbk. : alk. paper)
    1. Templo Mayor (Mexico City, Mexico)   2. Aztecs—Religion and
mythology.   3. Aztecs—Antiquities.   4. Mexico City (Mexico)—
Antiquities.   I. Title.
    F1219.1.M5M36813   1995
    972'.53—dc20   95-15700
                                             CIP

This book was set in ITC Usherwood.

10 9 8 7 6 5 4 3 2 1

13809507

LIFE A
TEMPI

The University Press of Colorado is pleased to present Eduardo Matos Moctezuma's *Life and Death in the Templo Mayor* as the second publication in the new series "Mesoamerican Worlds." This book by Mexico's finest archaeologist, who coordinated the astonishing excavation of the Templo Mayor from 1978 to 1982, explores the persuasive duality of Aztec religion and society, "coincidentia oppositorium" of life and death, war and agriculture, aggression and nurture at the ceremonial center of Tenochtitlan. Utilizing the offerings, sculpture, painted and written evidence, "Moctezuma Tercero," as he is affectionately called in Mexico, illuminates the ideology and cosmology of the place the Aztecs called the foundation of heaven. No one can do a better job of introducing us to the mighty Aztecs and the ways in which they symbolized their experiences in Mesoamerican worlds.

DAVÍD CARRASCO

Mesoamerican Worlds: From the Olmecs to the Danzantes

Contents

Preface

When we began the Templo Mayor Project in 1978, we knew how important it was to be able to penetrate and to understand in detail the main temple of the Mexica. It was a unique opportunity to break through the thick barrier of concrete that covers the city of Tenochtitlan and, archaeologically, to peer through the window of time and recover a time gone by. Archaeologists have in their hands the power to revive the dead and to come face to face with what used to be. In that way they confront the face of death and give it life.

Five years of work there allowed us to retrieve some of our history. Besides the Templo Mayor and its different building stages, we found a great quantity of archaeological materials that have now been studied by our collaborators at the Instituto Nacional de Antropología e Historia (INAH) and by researchers at other institutions who have shown interest in the topic. I acknowledge and thank them all. Of course, there are always scientific pirates who take advantage of the work of others, pretending to have done what they never did.

This book is the result of reflections on the symbolism of the Templo Mayor and its relationship to a stratified society like that of the Mexica. The path we will take through Nahuatl myths and through the Templo itself will allow us to approach the problem. We will not be satisfied just to stand before the excavated building and know that Tlaloc and Huitzilopochtli were on the upper level. We want to go beyond their presence, to penetrate time and space, to reach the phenomenon and the essence, to find out what the Templo Mayor really was.

Finally, I wish to dedicate this book to someone. As a rule, authors dedicate their works to certain persons. The beneficiaries are usually parents, a grandmother, a wife because of her patience, a secretary who had to copy and polish the work; there are many people to whom it could be dedicated. For my part, I wish to dedicate it to an anonymous person. I never knew his name, but he came almost daily to gaze through the cracks in the wall that protected the place to see what was coming out of the excavation. He was excited when he saw that something had been found, and he suffered if he saw that we were worried. I do not know what happened to him, but it is to him these pages are dedicated.

EDUARDO MATOS MOCTEZUMA
TLALPAN, AUGUST 1985

Translators' Note

All Nahuatl words are accented on the next to last syllable, therefore accents, which were used to indicate stress in Spanish, have been omitted except in direct quotations.

To avoid the errors involved in double translations, we often cite quotations from the original English version or from English translations from the original language, except for the *Códice Chimalpopoca* in Chapter 4, where the author preferred the Spanish version to Bierhorst's (1992) English translation.

We would like to thank our copy editor, Alice Colwell, for her meticulous work and her suggestions, which greatly improved the final product.

LIFE AND DEATH IN THE TEMPLO MAYOR

Basis for a Hypothesis

The excavations that were carried out for five years (1978–1982) in the center of Mexico City resulted in the recovery of several thousand objects associated with the Templo Mayor of Tenochtitlan. The importance of excavating in the site that was the most sacred of all for the Mexica was undeniable because it enabled us to enter into a context whose characteristics made it the place in which almost all the power, both real and symbolic, of that society was concentrated.[1]

In order to reach that goal, we used two disciplines that provided us with rich and varied information. These were written history and archaeology. Each one played a particular role in the investigation. The former consisted of the different sixteenth- and early-seventeenth-century chronicles, documents, and pictographs written by several chroniclers for various purposes. First were the soldier-chroniclers, who on many occasions sought to exalt the enterprise of conquest and to obtain privileges from the Crown. They were responsible for the Spanish victory, and their accounts were devoted for the most part to describing the

---

[1]. Matos Moctezuma 1978b.

entire process of the armed combat, although they also wrote interesting descriptions of other topics. This was true, for example, of Bernal
Díaz del Castillo, Hernán Cortés, and Tapia, all of whom referred directly
to the Templo Mayor, which they had seen, described, and finally
destroyed. There were also the chronicles written by the friars; among
those who stand out are Fray Bernardino de Sahagún, Motolinía, Torque-
mada, and others. It is interesting to note the friars' intention in collecting the characteristics of Mexica society in their original language;
Sahagún discussed it in the prologue to his monumental work *Historia
de las cosas de la Nueva España*:

> A doctor cannot properly give medicine to a patient without first know-
> ing from what humor or what cause each illness comes; therefore, a
> good doctor must be knowledgeable about medicines and diseases in
> order to prescribe the proper medicine for each ailment. Moreover,
> because the medical preachers and confessors must deal with souls in
> order to heal spiritual maladies, they must have experience with spiri-
> tual ailments and know their remedies. A preacher against the vices of
> the republic, in order to oppose them with his doctrine, and the confes-
> sor, in order to know what to ask and to understand what has to do with
> his office, must be aware of all that is needed to properly perform his
> duties. Neither should ministers be careless about their conversions, by
> stating that among those people the only sins are drunkenness, theft,
> and lust, because there are many more serious sins that cry out for rem-
> edy, sins of idolatry, pagan rituals, idolatrous superstitions and auguries,
> superstitions and ceremonies, which have not entirely disappeared.
>
> In order to preach against such things, and even to know about their
> existence, it is necessary to have knowledge of how they were used in
> the time of their idolatry; because if that is not known, they will con-
> tinue to do many idolatrous things in our presence, without our under-
> standing them. Some people say, in order to excuse themselves, that
> such things are only foolish or childish, since they are ignorant of the
> roots from which they originated, sheer idolatry; and the confessors
> do not ask about them nor think that they exist, since they do not
> speak the language necessary to inquire about them or even to under-
> stand them when they are told. Therefore, so that the evangelical min-
> isters who follow the ones who came first in the cultivation of this new

vineyard of the Lord, would not have a reason to complain about the first ones who left information about the natives of this New Spain hidden, I, Fray Bernardino de Sahagún, friar of the Order of Our Seraphic Father, Saint Francis, native of the village of Sahagún, in Campos, following the orders of the very Reverend Father, Fray Francisco Toral, provincial of this Province of the Santo Evangelio, and afterwards Bishop of Campeche and Yucatán, have written twelve books about divine things or, better said, about both the idolatrous and the human things of the natives of this New Spain.[2]

From this one can see that the friars were very interested in giving a precise idea of what their informants had told them, so that it might serve as a guide for the missionaries. This is important because it shows clearly, on the one hand, that they tried to make the data as reliable as possible and, on the other, that the mission of the church's penetration as an ideological apparatus of the Crown was to accomplish what force had failed to do—gain ideological control of the recently conquered groups. As we have said elsewhere, even though the friars had tried by various means to ameliorate the physical abuse of the natives by the *encomenderos* and other Spaniards, they did not give an inch when it came to imposing the new religion.[3]

A third group of chroniclers included Fernando Alvarado Tezozomoc, Fernando de Alva Ixtlilxochitl, and Chimalpahin, all of them natives whose works are of prime importance to our topic. One must also consider works like those of Alonso de Zorita, required reading because they dealt with specific areas that other sources do not mention or do so only in a general way. There are also some other manuscripts written in the Nahuatl language that have been translated, such as the "Anales de Cuauhtitlan" and the "Leyenda de los soles" that compose the so-called *Códice Chimalpopoca*, as well as the "Historia de los mexicanos por sus pinturas," to cite only a few.

All of these works make up a true body of information that gave us a basis for our theories about the Templo Mayor. However, a chronicler might have exaggerated what he was seeing or, to the contrary, adhered

---

[2.] Sahagún 1956, vol. 1: 25.
[3.] Matos Moctezuma 1978a.

too closely to what he was told, and we must also remember that an interpretation was given to the information at a particular moment. We must use such documentation cautiously, starting from the idea that the data must have been distorted to a greater or lesser degree but at the same time realizing that it is still usable material, as López Austin has suggested.[4] It is therefore necessary that the written source be corroborated by the other discipline whenever possible in order to verify the extent, truth, and value of the data it contains. Here archaeology is useful, allowing us to examine the Templo itself and to confront what was said in the sources. We can say that in this particular case most of the information we had was very close to what the archaeological data revealed. At the same time, once they are found, remains of this kind (and we have found very many of them, beginning in 1790 and extending through this century with the works of Leopoldo Batres,[5] Manuel Gamio,[6] Emilio Cuevas,[7] Hugo Moedano,[8] and the most recent works[9]) pose questions that can be resolved only by referring to the written sources. In this case the role is reversed, and it is archaeology that poses the problem to be solved and the sources that may provide the solution. In this way the two disciplines complement and help each other in the investigation.

Taking this into consideration, from the very beginning of the Templo Mayor Project, we set up the investigation according to three basic phases:

First Phase.   This consisted of collecting as much information as possible about the Templo Mayor, from both written and archaeological sources. On the basis of that information, we posed the problems to be

---

4. López Austin 1988.
5. See the anthology published by INAH as the first publication of the Templo Mayor Project, Matos Moctezuma 1979.
6. Matos Moctezuma 1979.
7. Matos Moctezuma 1979.
8. Matos Moctezuma 1979.
9. García Cook and Arana 1978. From the Templo Mayor Project, see Matos Moctezuma 1982b and Matos Moctezuma and Rangel 1982.

solved and established some of the categories we would use for the investigation. Some of the principal problems were of a general nature, and others were more specific. Among the first were the ones dealing with the gods we found on the top of the Templo: Tlaloc, god of rain, water, and fertility, and Huitzilopochtli, god of the sun, war, and the conquest of other groups. We concluded that the Templo Mayor was directly related to the economic requirements of the Mexica, since their economy depended fundamentally on certain aspects associated with these deities: on the one hand agricultural production and on the other war as a means of imposing tribute on conquered groups. In order to penetrate deeper into what that implied, we turned to two categories that would help us in the process of our investigation—*phenomenon* and *essence*. *Phenomenon* refers to the concrete aspect of the objects and the processes of their movable and changing objective reality, whereas *essence* is the internal and more stable aspect of the things or processes behind the phenomena manifested through them. Scientific research should be directed not only to the phenomena but especially to the internal processes, the essence, that directs them. Using that approach to the Templo and what it implied, we had before us what would be one of the basic features of the investigation: the structure-superstructure relationship. If the Templo Mayor was the expression of their fundamental needs for survival, in what way did the Mexica relate it to everything that had to do with religion, politics, and ideology, where much is expressed through symbolism in observable phenomena, such as the Templo Mayor itself, the characteristics of the festivities that took place there, the sacrifices, etc.? From that came further topics to investigate, one of which we will try to develop in this study.

Second Phase. The second phase of our investigation was the excavation, obtaining archaeological materials through a valid technique that would allow us to evaluate the information with the care and rigor it required. This phase lasted five years, during which we were able to obtain more than 7,000 archaeological objects, as well as the architectural data of the different building stages of the Templo Mayor. We will not repeat here the technical aspects of the excavation nor the most significant data we found, as we have done that in a general way in

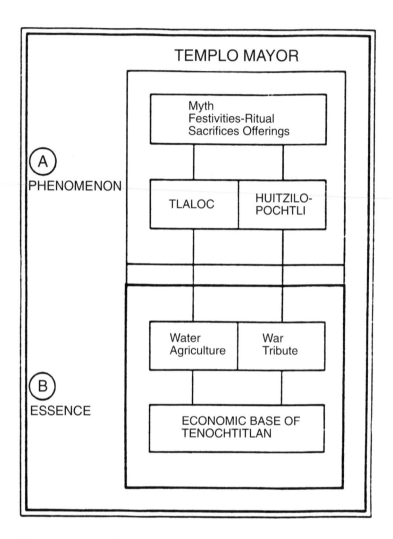

Phenomenon and essence in the Templo Mayor.

other publications.[10] Other interpretive studies of various aspects of the Templo Mayor were also prepared and published by the archaeological

---

[10.] See note 9.

team and other specialists of the INAH (biologists, chemists, conservators, etc.). It is enough for the present to point out that the wealth of material we obtained allowed us to know what the Templo Mayor was like and the importance it had from the perspectives mentioned above.

Third Phase.   This phase represents the union of the previous two, interpreting the material obtained, relating it to the historical sources, and comparing it to our initial proposals. We are now engaged in these matters, and this phase will take several years. There are, however, some topics in the interpretation that are directly related to what we have discussed above, and we will briefly outline one that particularly interests us because it is directly related to the symbolism of the Templo and its importance, both economic and ideological.

We have already mentioned the way in which the different chronicles referred to the Templo Mayor, its characteristics, and the gods in the two shrines in the upper part of the structure. There was also useful information about the festivities and the rituals that were performed there, as well as the importance of the Templo and its relationship to the myth of Huitzilopochtli's birth, as Seler studied these topics at the beginning of the century.[11] Various pictographs (Durán, Tovar, Sahagún, etc.) showed the Templo with its diverse attributes. Since 1790 and with greater frequency in this century the archaeological data that have been gathered through the work of several specialists—especially Gamio, Cuevas, Moedano, Archaeological Rescue, and more recently the Templo Mayor Project—have provided a greater wealth of architectural and sculptural elements, of movable objects proceeding (in the case of the Templo Mayor Project) from more than 100 offerings and from lesser buildings and shrines that were not described in the chronicles. All this data on archaeology, myth and ritual, and gods constitute a treasure trove to be examined in the light of new archaeological information.

One of the issues that immediately took on prime importance was establishing the symbolism of the Templo Mayor. Upon that depended other aspects, such as the presence of certain gods and the Templo's relationship to some of the most important myths, and these in turn

---

[11] Seler 1963.

were linked to the Mexica's vision of the universe. Citing studies of the religions developed by different societies in general and by the Mexica in particular, we concluded that the Templo Mayor represented the navel, the fundamental center of the Mexica universe, of their cosmovision. It was also the site where the vertical and the horizontal planes met, that is, the passage to the upper or celestial levels and to the underworld, and also the place from which the four directions of the universe departed. Moreover, not only was the Templo Mayor the center, but the building itself represented that cosmovision in its architectural components. Another important aspect of the Templo was that two of the principal Mexica myths were reenacted there in the form of sacred hills. The common denominator was in essence the need for the group's survival on the basis of agricultural production and war, elements present in many expressions of those myths. And there is something else: we assume that we are dealing with a stratified society, which means that ideology will acquire a particular significance in all the contexts.

Several important investigators have dealt with these topics as they relate to the Templo Mayor, and we will mention them as we proceed. We used the prior investigations in our study because we thought it would be helpful to assemble information that, far from exhausting the subject (which was not our intention), will open new paths and spawn ideas for future works that will evaluate or reject much of what has been said here.

In order to develop all of the above, we proceed in an orderly fashion. We begin by stating our position regarding the role of humans in the process of the development and creation of the gods; the importance of myth as an explanation for such phenomena as the Nahua concept of the universe; and, finally, how all of this is shown in the Templo Mayor of Tenochtitlan.

2

And Humans Created the Gods

From the earliest stages of the history of humankind, there has been a contradiction between humans and nature. Nature was modified to the degree that humans, in the process of their development and for the purpose of satisfying their needs, achieved better labor methods and perfected their tools on the basis of experience. Creators par excellence, humans not only produced those tools but also re-created nature itself through their art. Their creative power was such that it created the gods and left to them the power to make everything that surrounded them, including humanity itself. That was how humans explained the universe and their presence in it. Humans became the great makers of the gods. The great birth was accomplished. The gods of life and of death were born through the work and benevolence of humans, who made the gods just like themselves, with their weaknesses and strengths, their desires and passions, their struggles and problems, their life and death. That is, humans created the gods in their own image and likeness.

Humans were different from a god who rested on the seventh day of creation: they had to continue their production both in the physical as well as the spiritual realm. It should therefore not seem strange to us that throughout their history humans have made and perfected their technology and according to their needs expressed themselves artistically and changed the gods depending on circumstances. Let us look more closely at the creative process. There are three fundamental stages in the ancient history of humankind that allow us to follow the process of development and the way in which that process began. The first was an economy based on gathering, when humans took advantage of the resources that nature put within their reach and people essentially depended on hunting, fishing, and gathering wild fruit. Humans established their territory according to a constant observation of nature, which taught them the movements of animal species and the best places and best times for harvesting plants. They also used their inventiveness and experience to produce instruments to extend their reach and to perfect tactics for hunting and gathering within a communal organization, everyone collectively participating in those and other activities.

Their expressive power allowed them to fashion by means of their art a whole series of representations closely related to their needs. Several archaeological discoveries have placed at our disposal magnificent examples of the art of the European Upper Paleolithic, such as bone engravings, sculptures, and reliefs in rock and clay, as well as numerous cave pictographs. In all of them we see representations of animals, such as the reindeer, boar, mammoth, bull, bear, etc., which were indispensable as food, besides providing skins to wear as clothing and the materials needed to produce certain tools. What interests us most in these representations is how they were made.

There is no doubt that this creative ability manifested and was patterned on the needs of the group; in the case of the cave paintings they reveal something else: they were magnificently done by specialists in order to be successful in hunting. There were several reasons for this. One was the secretive character of the paintings. The artists chose not to paint at the entrance to the cave, where in some cases there were excellent stone walls upon which to paint; instead, they chose to paint the images in the deepest and darkest place in the cave. They were apparently looking for hidden places where the hunters could perform particular rituals. We have representations that seem to indicate practices of that kind. In *Les trois frères,* at Ariège, we see an individual painted black, wearing a skin and deer antlers, and carved in the rock in another part of that same place is a group in which another person dressed in a bison skin can be seen in front of some animals. Another find that seems to indicate such rituals is the cave of Montespan, Upper Garonne, where various clay sculptures depicting animals have been found; one was a headless bear on which was placed a real bear's head, its skull positioned between its front paws when the group was discovered. Also found here was an image of a horse that had about thirty wounds made by spears the hunters had thrown at it. In fact, we see that this truly magnificent paleolithic art was not done for the sake of art alone but was pursued for a practical purpose related to the survival of the group. Through artistic expression and the help of ritual, of the supernatural, humans sought means by which they could assure greater success for their own knowledge and technology.

Humans developed agriculture about 9,000 years ago. That advance, which arose out of the daily observation of nature, the cyclical change of seasons that leads to the birth and growth of plants, was of such importance that it revolutionized the very nature of society, from economics to religion. It is what Gordon Childe called the "Neolithic Revolution."[12] This real revolution in the process of development caused a qualitative change in the relationships of humans with nature as well as within the community itself. It signified an ever greater dependence on cultivated plants for survival and a change from an economy of gathering to one of production, which led to settlement as groups established themselves permanently in the first villages. This brought with it a new kind of social organization, although the same types of communal relationships were maintained among the members of the community. These were egalitarian agricultural societies. From that time on, the fertility of earth and water acquired fundamental importance, as the life of the group depended on them.

Humans deified those elements. Thus the earth, where plants were born, was converted into the great creative mother, as seen in the feminine portrayals of small clay figures generally related to fertility. And

---

[12.] Childe 1961.

water became the fertilizing element, the divine semen that gave life to plants. Humans had again created new gods.

Another qualitative change happened some millennia after that, with the appearance of the first stratified societies. Good examples are Egypt, Mesopotamia, and China, where such societies were fully developed around 3000 B.C. In America there were two areas in which this change took significant hold: the Andes and Mesoamerica. In the latter we see societies with those characteristics among the Olmecs around 1000 B.C.; from that time on, a specific mode of production developed throughout the area for 2,000 years, until the time of the Spanish conquest. We have already mentioned that for us the concept of Mesoamerica is equivalent to its mode of production. We have criticized Paul Kirchhoff[13] because in our judgment his characterization of Mesoamerica was based on traits he weighted equally, so that a fundamentally important economic element was placed on an equal plane with another referring to some peculiarity such as the use of sandals with heels. We also see that some of the traits he regarded as typically Mesoamerican were not found across the area but only in certain restricted zones. What we consider to be most important, however, is that he ignored the key characteristic of those societies: the presence of social classes and therefore of the state. In fact, many of the traits he mentioned were the result of that social organization.[14]

Several writers have tried to characterize those societies, and from this has come a topic that has provoked a great debate and to which a great many pages have been devoted, particularly among Marxists—the Asiatic mode of production. In his prologue to *A Contribution to the Critique of Political Economy*,[15] Marx mentioned it as a mode of production that preceded the ancient one; and in his *Pre-Capitalistic Economic Formations,* he presented some ideas on how it might be characterized. Subsequent studies have tried to sharpen the concept by using new information, but they have often simply led to greater confusion. Because we do not intend to go more deeply into the matter, we will

---

[13.] Kirchhoff 1943.
[14.] See Matos Moctezuma 1982a.
[15.] Marx 1970.

refer only to one of the last proposals that have been made about the early class societies, based on Felipe Bate's hypothesis.[16] We believe it opens new possibilities for understanding the first stratified society — indispensable to us as we analyze one such society.

The most relevant characteristic of the type of society with this mode of production — and what differentiates it from others — is that

> the ruling class owns the work force and, as in all precapitalist societies, has the ability to coerce the producers through extraeconomic means (ideological, political, and military), enabling it to control them effectively. It doesn't need to own the means of production, thus it makes no sense to claim that the extortion of a surplus is a form of rent of land.[17]

From the above we see that the ruling or exploiting class was characterized by its appropriation, either in services or products, of a given amount of work done by the exploited class. This leads us to assume that the ruling class actually owned the labor of the working class, whereas the latter owned the basic means of production: the earth, the tools, etc. Thus, the excess the ruling class appropriated appeared as tribute, either in services or products or, what is the same, in specie or labor. Here it should be added that tribute was given in two forms, internal and external. The former was obtained from people belonging to the group itself — in the case of the Mexica society, the *macehuales* [commoners] — while the latter was imposed on the conquered peoples.

In regard to the social division of work, we see that the ruling class monopolized all specialized knowledge and made it their own. What had formerly been owned by all the community was now the property of a sector of the society. It controlled astronomy, architecture, medicine, and other branches of knowledge. For its part, the exploited class was composed chiefly of farmers and artisans. It did the manual labor and was the work force that carried out collective construction projects, such as the building of temples, highways, and hydraulic works, and served in war.

[16.] Bate 1984.
[17.] Bate 1984.

The existence of these two classes was tied to the existence of the state, which regulated what was needed to ensure that the servitude persisted. We have described how the state used ideologies and coercive measures in order to maintain economic, political, social, and religious control.[18] One of the important aspects of social control was based on religion, which benefited the ruling class. The priest, possessor of knowledge of astronomy and seasonal changes as well as other learning, used his knowledge to make himself the intermediary between humans and the gods. The priest was the one who spoke to and appealed to the gods; he was their representative on earth. He and the ruler held the mandate of the gods, or, as often occurred, a single person represented both civil and religious powers. In this way skill and knowledge at the service of the ruling group were used to perfect the ideological and coercive instruments used to control society better.

Once again, the gods had been created in the likeness and image of the society in which they existed.

[18.] Matos Moctezuma 1979.

And Humans Created the Myths

In the most remote past, humans built a supernatural world that had many of the events they had observed in nature. They created gods who in their turn gave life to everything that existed and constructed the universal order according to human knowledge and experience.

Explanations of the phenomena humans saw around them can be found in myths; myths answered all the principal problems humans faced. Researchers have devoted many pages to the analysis and interpretation of myths. There are investigators who contend that humans arrived at those explanations through false thought processes. Some say that Western logic is different from that of so-called primitive peoples. Others say that science and myth are equally valid explanations, while still others deny that myths pursue any immediate or practical objective.

Because we stated our ideas about this in part in the preceding chapter, we will not go into the details of those different schools of thought here but will only point out some aspects related to myth as a form of explanation and a means of communication through myth-ritual relationships. That will be useful to us later.

If we analyze what scholars say on the topic, we find that despite some controversy, they agree on certain relationships. According to Mauss and Hubert,[19] myths are established in space and are produced in time through rituals that represent a reenactment of the former. Lévi-Strauss,[20] one of the authors who tried to analyze the structure of myths, pointed out that they always refer to past events. He posed the question why identical or similar myths exist in different parts of the world. We are indebted to him for a technique for analyzing myths that starts by breaking them down into their constituent mythemes. According to Jensen,[21] myth and ritual are closely connected. He said that in many cases acts of worship are representations of the corresponding myths. For his part, Mircea Eliade[22] made an important contribution by joining time and space in a relevant manner. He said that there are two kinds of time, the sacred and the profane. The former is a circular, reversible time that can be retrieved by means of ritual. In this way events in the distant past (myth) are reenacted through ritual.

We can add to that. Some myths were created or derived from real historical events. What was a conflict among humans can be converted into a conflict between gods; if a human or a cultural hero was involved, he could, if necessary, be changed into a god. As a result we have an important cycle: first there is a real, historical event that people want to preserve because of its importance, and they explain it through myth. This is how the second step arises: myth is created as an explanation. There is often the need to have a myth last over time, and rituals are the means to accomplish this. It should be pointed out that this is not the way all myths begin. We refer to particular myths related to the birth of some gods and, occasionally, to humanity itself.

We can see that myth and ritual are intimately related and that the latter, among other roles, serves as a means of communication between the society in which it is performed and those who want to control it. In

---

[19.] Mauss and Hubert 1970.
[20.] Lévi-Strauss 1963.
[21.] Jensen 1963.
[22.] Eliade 1958.

these cases the myth-ritual relationship is expressed ideologically by the context in which it occurs.

What are some of the most common myths across societies? In order to answer that question, we propose a fourfold classification that corresponds to the principal myths related to the genesis (or the beginning) of gods, the universe, and the life and death of beings, although other classifications may exist. It is also important to point out that several types of myths can be seen within the same account. *Theogonic* myths refer to the origin of the gods. In many cases these are creator gods who have existed throughout eternity and sometimes acquire the characteristics of the god Eliade called Ociosus, a god represented only by symbols whose function was to create other gods and who was not specifically worshiped. These myths can also refer to gods deriving from a cultural hero or an important personage who was later deified. The number of gods and their origins may vary according to the kind of society involved and its characteristics. *Cosmogonic* myths are related to the birth or the beginning of the universe, the heavenly bodies, and their remotest origins. *Anthropogenic* myths tell of the birth or creation of humans. In general they are central to all other myths; in other words, all of creation is related to humans themselves. Finally, there are the *necrogenic* myths, so named because they refer to what happens to humans after death and the places to which they will go, as well as to the gods that preside over those places. Death is a constant, undeniable, and inevitable occurrence. When faced with death and loss of existence, humans, the great makers of the gods, sought to transcend that fate in some way and resorted to their creative power to invent something after death, assuring their survival.

Nahua Myths

Our study focuses on one of the Nahua groups about which we have rich and varied information from both archaeological and historical sources: the Aztecs, or Mexica, whom we consider to be the heirs of the Nahua groups who preceded them in the Valley of Mexico. It should be pointed out that *Nahua* is a generic term that includes several groups who spoke the Nahuatl language and who were present in the Valley of

Mexico and surrounding areas from the ninth century A.D. and perhaps even before. Among them were the Toltec, Chichimec, Tepanec, etc., all of whom had in common certain aspects of their economy as well as their society and religion, although of course they possessed and expressed their own peculiarities.

The Nahua myths we relate here are of primary importance to the purpose of this book: to understand both how the Templo Mayor became the center of the universal order and how some of the myths were reenacted in the temple, making it a living myth. To do this in an orderly way, we begin with a myth that tells about Mexica cosmovision, as this is indispensable to our understanding the place the temple held in the order of their universe.

Mexica Cosmovision

The Nahua explained the universal order according to their knowledge of nature. This cosmovision was a corpus of ideas and thoughts, a structured ordering of the place the gods, astral bodies, earth, and humans themselves held in the universe, and the explanations derived from them.[23]

Several studies concur in relating Nahua cosmovision. In the "Historia de los mexicanos por sus pinturas," there is a very important myth that contains several references that allow us to introduce the topic we are developing here. The account relates:

> Six hundred years after the birth of the four brother gods, the sons of Tonacatecli (Tonacatecuhtli), all four of them met and said that it was fitting that they ordain what had to be done and what order it must have; and all of them agreed that Quetzalcóatl and Uchilobi (Huitzilopochtli) would be the ones to arrange it. By the agreement and order of the other two, those two then made fire, and when that was done, they made a half sun, which, because it was not complete, shed only a little light. Then they made a man and a woman. They called the man Uxumuco (Oxomoco), and they gave the name of Cipastonal (Cipactónal) to the woman. They ordered them to cultivate the earth and told her to

---

[23.] There are several definitions of the concept; see López Austin 1988, vol. 1: 12–18.

spin and weave. They also said that they would give birth to the *macehuales* and that they must not be idle but always work. The gods gave her certain grains of corn so that she could heal, make use of prophecies, and practice witchcraft. Women still do that today. Then they made the days and divided them into months, giving each one twenty days, and 360 days to the year, as will be told later. They then made Mitlitlatteclet (Mictlantecuhtli) and Michitecaciglat (Mictecacíhuatl), husband and wife. They were gods of hell, and they put the couple in it. Then they created the heavens beyond the thirteenth, and they created water, and in it they created a big fish called *cipoa cuacli* (Cipactli), which was like an alligator, and from that fish they made the earth, as will be related. . . .[24]

Several things can be derived from this account, for instance, the *theogonic* myth, with the constant presence of the dual principle from which the creator gods emerged. Tonacatecuhtli (Lord of Our Sustenance) and his feminine counterpart, Tonacacihuatl, form the fundamental dual principle, Ometeotl. It was also identified with the old god and with the god of fire (Huehueteotl-Xiuhtecuhtli), who occupied the center of the universe in all of its levels. Sahagún expressed it thus:

> Mother of the gods, father of the gods, the old god,
> spread out on the navel of the earth
> within the circle of turquoise,
> He who dwells in the waters the color of the bluebird,
> he who dwells in the clouds.
> The old god, he who inhabits the shadows of the land of the dead,
> the Lord of fire and of time.[25]

In his *Aztec Thought and Culture,* León Portilla analyzed this text, which begins by naming the masculine-feminine duality of the old god (Huehueteotl), who was the creator of the gods, as indicated in the previous myth. We see clearly that this duality applied to the center (the navel) of the earth, of the waters and the clouds (celestial levels, heavens), as well as of the region of the dead—that is to say, the three levels of the Nahua cosmovision.

[24.] "Historia de los mexicanos por sus pinturas" 1941.
[25.] Taken from León Portilla 1963: 32.

That dual principle created the four creator gods: Quetzalcoatl and the three Tezcatlipocas. It was they who with their struggles and alternations created the suns, or the ages, of the world. In the account we can see the sequence in which things were created. They made fire, made a half sun, and formed the initial human couple, Cipactonal and Oxomoco, giving them some grains of corn and teaching them to sow and weave. This is interesting because people such as the Mexica depended to a large extent upon agricultural production. Next came something notable in that they created time, with days, months, and, finally, years. They created the solar calendar, which was based on the changes in nature itself. Finally, they created the upper levels (celestial) and the lower ones (underworld) and earth itself.

It is worthwhile to analyze some of the myths elements. We will begin with the four creator gods, the ones who, according to what we know, ruled over the four directions of the universe. There was a struggle among them that produced the cyclical movement with the appearance of the different suns, or ages, as we see in the "Leyenda de los soles," which we analyze later. It is not surprising that *ollin* (movement) was represented by four windmill vanes, which may very well symbolize each one of these directions and gods. Out of the constant struggle among the Tezcatlipocas and Quetzalcoatl, all of creation emerged.

We will not take the time here to study the creation of fire, the sun, and the first couple, since we examine them more thoroughly later on. But it is absolutely necessary to discuss the creation of the calendar and, afterward, the levels that composed the Nahua worldview.

It is logical that the year was generally divided into eighteen months of twenty days each, corresponding to the needs of a bellicose agricultural people, since the festivities and rituals celebrated throughout the year were tied to the activities that formed the economical underpinning of Tenochtitlan. Regarding this calendar, Durán said, "Such images served these nations by letting them know the days they had to sow and plow the earth, cultivate the corn, remove weeds, harvest, remove the grain from the cobs, and sow beans and chia, keeping track each month so many days after such a factor or such a date."[26]

[26.] Durán 1967.

A list of the months and the gods to whom they were dedicated, according to Sahagún, allows us to see this more clearly:

1. Atlcahualo—It began February 2 and was dedicated to the *tlaloques* [Rain God helpers]; to Chalchiuhtlicue, the goddess of water; and to Quetzalcoatl.
2. Tlacaxipehualiztli—It began February 22 and was dedicated to Xipe Totec. Captives were flayed in a possible ritual of renewal.
3. Tozoztontli—Dedicated to Tlaloc, in order to attract rain. It corresponded to parts of March and April, the months preceding the rainy season.
4. Uey Tozoztli—In honor of Centeotl, goddess of corn, and of Chicomecoatl.
5. Toxcatl—Dedicated to Tezcatlipoca. In this month a young man representing the god was sacrificed.
6. Etzalcualiztli—In honor of Tlaloc and the *tlaloques*. Slaves wearing the apparel of the latter were sacrificed.
7. Tecuilhuitontli—Dedicated to Uixtocihuatl, sister of the *tlaloques*. It corresponded in part to the month of June.
8. Uey Tecuilhuitl—Dedicated to Xilonen, goddess of the green corn, which grew in that month.
9. Tlaxochimaco—In honor of Huitzilopochtli, god of war, and to other deities related to death. This month was also known by the name of Miccailhuiltontli, or the small feast of the dead. It corresponded to the month of July.
10. Xocotl Huetzi—Dedicated to Xiuhtecuhtli, god of fire.
11. Ochpaniztli—In honor of Toci, mother of the gods. Huitzilopochtli was also honored, as well as neophyte warriors. It corresponded in part to August and September.
12. Teotleco—In honor of the arrival of all the gods. It corresponded to the last twenty days of September.
13. Tepeilhuitl—Feasts in honor of the hills, where the clouds were formed (related to water deities). It corresponded in part to October.
14. Quecholli—Dedicated to Mixcoatl. Spears were made for war. It corresponded in part to October and November.

15. Panquetzaliztli—Feast in honor of Huitzilopochtli, god of war.
16. Atemoztli—In honor of Tlaloc and the *tlaloques*. The greater part
    of it corresponded to December. It was said that in this month it
    began to thunder and "to show signs of rain."
17. Tititl—In honor of Tona, "our mother." Ceremonies were
    performed in the Templo Mayor. Related to war.
18. Izcalli—Dedicated to Xiuhtecutli, god of fire. The new fire was lit
    in the middle of the month. It corresponded in part to January.
    After the last day of that month came the five *nemontemi* days,
    considered to be unfortunate.

If we notice the manner in which these months were distributed
throughout the year and the deities to whom they were dedicated, we
see clearly that they were closely related to, among other things, three
fundamental aspects: agriculture, war, and fire. We can also see that the
first three months were related to preparations to attract rain, the
renewal. The fourth month, Uey Tozoztli, was when the rainy season
began. Months six, seven, and eight were when the corn was in full
growth, thus the feast of Xilonen took place in the last month. The ninth
month was dedicated to war, to death. Then came the preparations for
death and the harvesting of the plants. As the end of the rainy season
approached, there were more feasts in honor of fire, Xiuhtecuhtli, and of
war, Huitzilopochtli, or of deities linked to the latter, such as the mother
goddess, who was worshiped in the Templo Mayor. War brought about
the conquest of other regions and yielded the tributes imposed on the
conquered groups. Thus the dry season had its reward in tribute, the
product of war. We can see the relationship between the festivities dedicated to war or to fire and the dry season, as in the case of months
eleven, fourteen, fifteen, seventeen, and eighteen.

If we continue our analysis of the myth, we come to a very important part: the creation of the three levels of the universe. The account is
clear. We see the creation of Mictlantecuhtli and Mictlancihuatl, the rul-
ers of Mictlan, the place of the dead—in other words, the lower level
and the underworld. Afterward the thirteen heavens, or celestial levels,
were created, then water and Cipactli (alligator), which in turn became

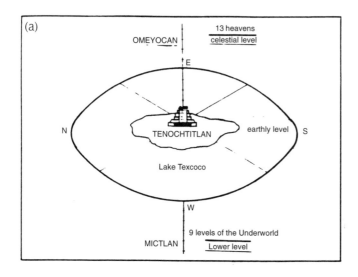

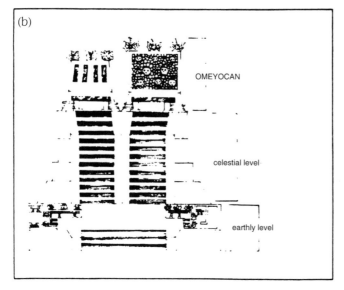

a. Nahua levels of the universe; b. Levels of the universe represented in the Templo Mayor.

the earth. Below we give more details about each of these three levels, beginning with an explanation of their location.

The structure of the Nahua universe consisted of two planes, one vertical and the other horizontal. The place where both planes intersected was the center, the navel that formed one of the three levels, the earth. That terrestrial level divided vertical space into two parts: above was the celestial level, and below the underworld. On each of these was located the dual principle, Ometeotl.

Terrestrial Level

This level formed the horizontal plane. From its center came the four directions of the universe, which were identified with each of the creator gods, each having a specific symbol and color. The latter could vary in different versions. Thus the east, Tlapallan, whose symbol was a reed, corresponded to the red Tezcatlipoca. The north was ruled by the black Tezcatlipoca, and it was the region of Mictlampa, of the dead. Its symbol was flint. The blue Tezcatlipoca, actually Huitzilopochtli, the god of sun and war, corresponded to the south, Huitztlampa, whose symbol was the rabbit. Finally, Quetzalcoatl, the wind god, was found in the west, called Cihuatlampa. Its color was white, and its symbol was the *calli* (house). These directions were also identified with specific plants, as can be seen in the Códice Borgia. Their key function was to hold up the sky and, together with the center, to act as channels by which the gods could descend to earth.[27]

The center, or navel, of those four directions, where the vertical and the horizontal planes crossed, was located in the Templo Mayor of Tenochtitlan. That was the reason for its great sanctity. Similarly, the city of Tenochtitlan was located in the middle of a lake, which corresponded to the concept of *cemanahuac,* the idea that land was surrounded by water, the turquoise ring. The Mexica's city of origin, Aztlan, was also located in the middle of a lake and was surrounded by water. In a larger sense the coasts and the sea were the outer limits of that concept. There

[27.] See López Austin 1988, vol. 1: 58–61.

is no doubt that the Mexica thus claimed to be the center of the universe, the chosen people.

The terrestrial level was the place inhabited by humans. From the struggle of the cosmic forces of the four gods began the dialectical process that gave birth to the ages, or suns, and the presence of humankind on the earth. Universal equilibrium was achieved on the basis of that constant dialectic.

Celestial Level

This level was formed by the thirteen heavens, although occasionally nine or ten are mentioned. For example, nine heavens were mentioned at the moment when a child was born and the midwife bathed it, saying, "Our most pious lady, Chalchiuhtlicue, or Chalchiuhtlatonac, this, your servant, has come here into this world, whom our mother and our father, who are called Ometecutli and Omecihuatl and who live above the nine heavens, the dwelling place of those gods, have sent. We do not know what gifts he brings."[28]

This does not contradict what we will see later, since the place gods resided was beyond the ninth heaven. The observation of the stars and their movements led to determining the different heavens and is portrayed in the Códice Vaticano A 3738. The first of those heavens was the place where the moon and the clouds were found, which everyone could see. The stars were in the second, and it was also known as the Citlalco. The stars were divided into two great groups, those of the north, called Centzon mimixcoa, which means the countless of the north, and the Centzonhuitznahua, the countless of the south. The third was the one through which the sun passed on his daily round, while the fourth was where Venus was found, or, in another interpretation, Uixtocihuatl, the goddess of brackish salty waters, sister of the *tlaloques*.[29] The fifth corresponded to the place where the comets passed, or the heaven where gyration occurred. The

---

[28.] Sahagún 1956.

[29.] López Austin (1988, vol. 1: 54–61) has some proposals concerning the Códice Vaticano A 3738.

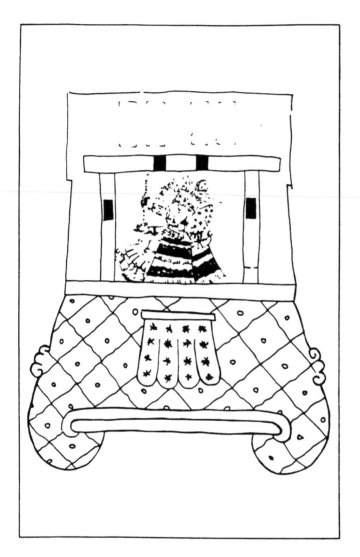

Tlaloc's temple atop a hill (*Códice Borbónico*).

next two heavens were represented with colors: they could be green and blue or black and blue. The eighth heaven was characterized as the place where tempests were formed, the Iztapalnacazcayan, which means "place that has corners made of obsidian slabs." The three that followed were thought to be the place of the gods, and the last two were the place of duality, the Omeyocan.[30]

Lower Level (The Underworld)

This level was located under the earth, and as in the thirteen heavens just described, there were nine places or passages to cross before arriving at the deepest one, the Mictlan or Chicunauhmictlan, according to Sahagún. Several researchers have been interested in one aspect of this level, that is, the relationship of Mictlan, the underworld, and the region of the north, the Mictlampa, the direction of the dead. Yet it is important to remember that the sun, called Tzontemoc when it set in the west, entered the world of the dead, so that we see three cardinal directions related to death in some way. Perhaps that explains what Seler[31] pointed out in his study of the Códice Borgia: that the four directions were also found in the world of the dead.

Another important aspect is what happens to the body and to the soul, or *teyolia,* of the deceased. We must first understand the role played by the earth as the place where corpses remained. It is clear that the bodies of the dead, whether incinerated or buried, were placed in the earth. Another important aspect was that the earth, the great mother goddess represented by Coatlicue and other feminine deities, took the bodies of the deceased into her bosom no matter how they died. This property was also attributed to the masculine counterpart, the god Tlaltecuhtli, the earth monster, who was portrayed as a being with great, open, fanged jaws and clawed hands and feet, and usually adorned with skulls and curly hair like the gods of death. His role, to be fed human bodies, was often mentioned at the time of an individual's birth as well as the time of his death in war. The midwife, speaking to the newborn child would say, "Your own land is another one; you are promised elsewhere, and that is the field where wars are waged, where battles are fought. You are sent there; your office and your purpose is war; your

---

[30.] Concerning the Omeyocan, see León Portilla 1963.
[31.] Seler 1963.

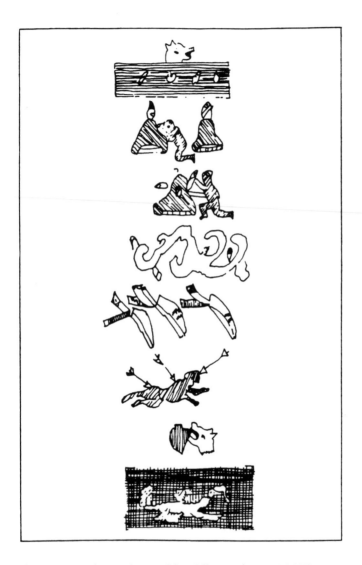

The route to the underworld (*Códice Vaticano A 3738*).

destiny is to give drink to the sun with the blood of the enemies and to feed the earth, called 'Tlaltecuhtli,' with the bodies of your enemies."[32]

[32.] Sahagún 1956.

The same plea — to succeed in war — can be seen in the prayers addressed to Tezcatlipoca, in which all of the above were again mentioned:

> The earth god opens his mouth, thirsty to drink the blood of the many who will die in this war. It seems that the sun and the earth god called Tlaltecuhtli want to celebrate. They will give food and drink to the gods of heaven and of hell, inviting them to partake of the flesh and blood of the men who will die in this war. The gods of heaven and of hell await to see who will win . . . whose blood will be drunk and whose flesh will be eaten.[33]

The first citation shows clearly that the sun was to be nourished with blood, while the earth was fed with the blood and the body, the mortal remains of the warriors, because the body or the ashes had to be deposited in the earth.

Of course the known sculptures of Tlaltecuhtli were not intended to be visible, as the relief with the figure of the god was always turned downward toward the earth. We mention this for several reasons. In the first place, the sculpture of the mother goddess Coatlicue had a representation of that god facing downward on the base. This led Humboldt[34] to believe that the sculpture ought to be raised, so that the image could be seen. His Western bias prevented him from understanding that it was important for the native that the earth deity face downward. In the excavations at the Templo Mayor, several sculptures of this god were found, usually in a colonial column, something we had already seen in similar pieces exhibited in the Museo Nacional de Antropología. The explanation is clear. The conquered natives were the ones who prepared the architectural components of the first colonial buildings, no doubt under the direction of friars or European masons. We know that the natives tried to preserve their beliefs and idols, and in a moment of negligence on the part of the Spaniards, they buried their images in the walls or foundations of the new building. Let us imagine the Mexica quarryman reworking an ancient image of Tlaltecuhtli as the base for a column. He

---

[33.] Sahagún 1956.
[34.] Humboldt 1891.

would skip working the face where the image was. He knew that the god should be placed downward and would spare the side with the image. In answer to the Spaniard's question why he didn't cut off that part, the native would answer that it was not necessary because it would face downward and would not be visible. The Spaniard believed him and went on, the Indian succeeding in his intention of placing the god in its correct position. What a flimsy base for the colonial foundations!

It is apparent from the above that the body or ashes would remain in the earth, nourishing Tlaltecuhtli, but the *teyolia,* a kind of soul of the individual, would go to the place provided for it, the same as the other elements of the person.[35] We know that there were three specific places to go, depending on the nature of death as well as the kind of burial. We have spoken of this on another occasion,[36] but it is worth repeating briefly. One of the places the *teyolia* went was the house of the sun. Accompanying the sun on a part of his path was a privilege given to those who had died in combat or as sacrifices and to women who had died while giving birth to their first children, as childbirth was also considered to be a battle involving the capture of an enemy. The midwife would say to a woman dying in her first childbirth,

> strong and valiant woman, my beloved daughter! Brave woman, beautiful and tender dove, my lady, you have labored and toiled bravely; you have conquered. You have done as your mother did, the lady Cihuacoatl, or Quilaztli. You have fought bravely. With strength and confidence, you have used the shield and the sword placed in your hands by your mother, the lady Cihuacoatl, Quilaztli.[37]

Warriors were entitled to accompany the sun from dawn until noon and women from noon until sunset. Warriors were guaranteed passage to life after death, since at the end of four years they would be converted into birds with beautiful plumage and would sip the nectar of flowers. For that reason, in Nahua poetry death in war, death by the obsidian

---

35. López Austin 1988, vol. 1: 318–321.
36. Matos Moctezuma 1978.
37. Sahagún 1956.

edge, is desirable. Of course that concept of a warrior's destiny conformed to the ideological position of a society that required warriors for its survival.

Another destination was Tlalocan, which was conceived to be a place of constant summer, always green with fruits and plants. It was the place of Tlaloc, the god of rain, of water. People who had died in some way related to water—those who drowned, had dropsy, were struck by lightning, etc.—went there.

Finally, people who died a natural death went to Mictlan, but in order to do so, the souls of the deceased had to traverse nine places or levels. Sahagún[38] listed some of them: two colliding mountains; the place where a serpent guarded a path; the place of the green lizard; eight cold, windy plains and eight hills; the place of the razorlike cold wind; the place of the crossing of the river Chicunauhapan and arrival at Mictlan.

According to the version in the Códice Vaticano A 3738, the places were the following: "the earth, the passageway for water, the place where the hills collide, obsidian hill, place of the obsidian wind, place where banners wave, place where people are pierced with arrows, place where people's hearts are devoured, obsidian place of the dead, place with no outlet for smoke."[39]

The first question that comes to mind is: Why were there nine stages? Several authors have tried to answer the question in different ways, relating it to night and to the "lords of night" or to a week divided into nine days[40] or to a day composed of nine periods of time.[41] We have a hypothesis that we believe is supported by various elements in the schema. The nine steps that an individual who died a natural death traveled represented a return to the maternal womb (the earth) from which life emerged. Let us recall that opposed to the nine celestial levels, which were masculine (from them came heat and rain, or divine semen), the earth was a feminine deity from whose interior plants were

---

[38.] Sahagún 1956.
[39.] López Austin 1988, vol. 1: 55.
[40.] Nowotny 1961.
[41.] González Torres 1975.

born. The Mexica, like other people, knew that when menstruation stopped nine times, it was a sign that a woman was pregnant and that the result was the birth of a child. But prior to that a fountain of water came out, an inner spring (amniotic fluid). The inside of the womb was a dark place, without windows, just like Mictlan. Thus it was not unusual for a corpse to be placed with its legs bent, to be buried in what specialists call the fetal position, and for the body to be sprinkled with water. It was a form of returning to the same position and ambience it had before birth. Moreover, there is evidence that caves, the interior of the earth, were perceived as wombs that could give birth to individuals or to groups of people. Chicomoztoc, or the seven caves, was portrayed as a womb in the *Historia Tolteca-Chichimeca*.[42] The walls of caves are depicted in the same way used to indicate skin in other pre-Hispanic figures. Moreover, a passage in the account is very explicit in this respect. This is the moment in which the Toltec envoys arrived at Chicomoztoc, or Colhuacatepec, and spoke to one another:

> And for the second time, he said to Quetzalteueyac, "My pilli, tlatouani Quetzalteueyac, look, strike the cave, the Coliuhquitepetl. Yes! Let us complete our task! We are making our creator and maker suffer!" Then Quetzalteueyac struck the cave, the hill, and broke the edge of the cave. Quetzalteueyac took as a second name that of Uitec (beater). And this happened two and a half days after their arrival in Colhuacatepec.[43]

A footnote by the editors elucidates the meaning (correctly, in our judgment): "We believe that the act of striking the cave refers here to an act of creation, the primordial act of striking and opening the earth so that a human being could emerge from it."

Placing human remains in jars was also considered to be a return to the original cave, the womb.[44]

Summing up our proposition, we see that the darkness, the water, the individual's position, etc. derived from the anatomical and physiological

---

[42] Kirchhoff, Güemes, and Reyes García 1976.
[43] Kirchhoff, Güemes, and Reyes García 1976.
[44] Heyden 1981.

knowledge the Mexica had acquired, which related life and death in a significant way. The path that gave life and stopped blood on nine different occasions was employed in a reverse sense to reintegrate the deceased to the maternal womb, which is the earth. We believe this explains many things.

The concept of nine places, or underworlds, and of the same number of heavens (or more) is also present in the Western world. Whoever has read Dante's *Divine Comedy* will remember that the journey of the poet, accompanied by Virgil, to the infernal regions, to purgatory, and to the heavens has much in common with the concepts in the Nahua world. The poem, written about A.D. 1300,[45] begins with the two traveling to the nine regions of hell. There are several similarities besides those mentioned previously, such as the need to cross a river, the Acheron, in order to get to Hades, which resembles the need to pass through Apanahuayan, "the passageway for water" in the Códice Vaticano A 3738 version. The presence of a dog is also important, although it played different roles. In the case of the third hell, the dog Cerberus tormented the spirits residing there, whereas among the Nahua the dog assisted in crossing the river. We also recall that Dante tells about the second and third infernos that had hurricanes and hail; the Nahua had the cold obsidian wind. The similarities in the heavens are also very significant. The first heaven in both versions was the moon. For Dante, the second one was the planet Mercury; for the Nahua, the place of the stars. The third one was Venus for Dante and the sun for the Nahua, whereas the fourth was the reverse. In the fifth through the seventh, Dante's heavens were the planets; the eighth was the stars; and the ninth contained all the heavens. From there on was the place of the gods, up to the highest level of divine contemplation. For the Nahua, the ninth was also the place of the gods, until the thirteenth level, where the supreme duality resided.

The similarity is astonishing. It seems logical, however, that the observation of the astral bodies gave access to the heavens, and the versions of hell, or the underworld, were spoken of in related terms,

---

[45.] Dante 1970.

4

And Humans Created the Humans

Now that we have examined Nahua cosmovision, we need to explore other myths that complement what we have already said and will reinforce our presentation of the Templo Mayor. They also serve as examples of the four classes of myths mentioned previously, as well as others. To do this, we refer to myths originally written in the Nahuatl language that are included in what is known as the "Leyenda de los soles." This manuscript is dated 1558 and, together with the "Anales de Cuauhtitlan," is part of the so-called *Códice Chimalpopoca* (given that name by the abbot Brasseur de Bourbourg in honor of one of the first translators of the document, Faustino Galicia Chimalpopoca). We are especially interested in the part known as the "Leyenda de los soles" (so called by Francisco del Paso y Troncoso) because, in a single account, it contains several myths referring to what we have mentioned before. We keep to the original order in presenting the myths, but we deal with each act of creation separately in order to comment on it.

I.   Founding of the Earth

Here is the oral account of what is known of how the earth was founded long ago.

One by one, here are its various foundations [ages].

How it began, how the first Sun had its beginning 2513 years ago — thus it is known today, the 22 of May, 1558.

This Sun, 4-Tiger, lasted 676 years.

Those who lived in this first Sun were eaten by ocelots. It was the time of the Sun 4-Tiger.

And what they used to eat was our nourishment, and they lived 676 years.

And they were eaten in the year 13.

Thus they perished and all ended. At this time the Sun was destroyed.

It was on the year 1-Reed. They began to be devoured on a day [called] 4-Tiger. And so with this everything ended and all of them perished.

This Sun is known as 4-Wind.

Those who lived under this second Sun were carried away by wind. It was under the Sun 4-Wind that they all disappeared.

They were carried away by the wind. They became monkeys.

Their homes, their trees — everything was taken away by the wind.

And this Sun itself was also swept away by the wind.

And what they used to eat was our nourishment.

[The date was] 12-Serpent. They lived [under this Sun] 364 years.

Thus they perished. In a single day they were carried off by the wind. They perished on a day 4-wind.

The year [of this Sun] was 1-Flint.

This Sun, 4-Rain was the third.

Those who lived under this third Sun, 4-Rain, also perished. It rained fire upon them. They became turkeys.

This Sun was consumed by fire. All their homes burned.

They lived under this Sun 312 years.

They perished when it rained fire for a whole day.

And what they used to eat was our nourishment.

[The date was] 7-Flint. The year was 1-Flint and the day 4-Rain.

They who perished were those who had become turkeys.

The offspring of turkeys are now called *pipil-pipil.*

This Sun is called 4-Water; for 52 years the water lasted.

And those who lived under this fourth Sun, they existed in the time of the Sun 4-Water.

It lasted 676 years.

Thus they perished: they were swallowed by the waters and they became fish.

The heavens collapsed upon them and in a single day they perished.

And what they ate was our nourishment.

[The date was] 4-Flower. The year was 1-House and the day 4-Water.

They perished, all the mountains perished.

The water lasted 52 years and with this ended their years.

This Sun, called 4-Movement, this is our Sun, the one in which we now live.

And here is its sign, how the Sun fell into the fire, into the divine hearth, there at Teotihuacán.

It was also the Sun of our Lord Quetzalcóatl in Tula.

The fifth Sun, its sign 4-Movement.

[It] is called the Sun of Movement because it moves and follows its path.

And as the elders continue to say, under this sun there will be earthquakes and hunger, and then our end shall come.[46]

We consider this myth to be very important because it reflects much of the Nahua concept of the universe. Although there are about ten versions of the myth that still await study in depth, we believe this version is adequate for our purpose. First, we want to point out some important elements because it is a myth that tells of the various attempts of the gods to establish the earth, to create humans, and to endow them with food. But it goes even further: it involves the Nahua cosmovision of the universal order, achieved through creation-destruction, the result of conflicts among the gods. We saw previously in the "Historia de los mexicanos por sus pinturas" the theogonic myth of the birth of the four gods, sons of the principle of duality, but if we examine the myth carefully, we see that everything was related to the presence of humans on earth and providing them with nourishment to sustain them. In this way each new sun, or age, was created and was in its turn destroyed by diverse elements that can be identified with each one of these gods. What stands out in the struggle is the dualism, the fundamental basis for all cosmic happenings. Life and death, creation and destruction, were present. However, we emphasize that the whole myth shows not only the gods' need to establish the earth correctly in order for the equilibrium of the universe to be perfect but also how they were directed toward accomplishing this through the presence of humans. What is important here is

---

[46.] Version taken from León Portilla 1963: 38–39; line numbers have been removed. The remaining citations are from *Códice Chimalpopoca* 1945, including the reference to the "Anales de Cuauhtitlan."

that only the presence of humans and the food the gods provided justi-
fied the gods' conflicts and adventures. The objective of the battle
between Tezcatlipoca and Quetzalcoatl was for the humans each created to prevail on earth, but each creation was destroyed by the other.
Thus the struggle went back and forth in the effort to establish humans
on earth and attain the universal equilibrium — a very difficult goal, as
we will see later.

II.   Creation of Fire

When their year was ending, Titlacahuan called out to the one named
Tata and to his wife, Nene, and he said to them, "Don't ask for anything
else. Dig a hole in a very large *ahuehuetl* [Mexican bald cypress] and go
inside when the time (Toçoçtli) comes, when the sky comes crashing
down." They went in. Then he shut them inside and said to them, "You
and your wife will eat only one ear of corn apiece." When they had
eaten all of the kernels, they noticed that the water was receding and
that the trunk was no longer moving. They removed the cover and saw
a fish. They built a fire with the fire drill (threw on the torch), and
roasted the fish for themselves. The gods Citlallinicue and Citlallatonac
glanced that way and said, "Gods, who has made a fire? Who has filled
the sky with smoke?" Titlacahuan, Tezcatlipoca came down at once,
scolded them, and said, "What are you doing, Tata?" Then he cut their
throats and put their heads on their behinds, turning them into dogs.

The sky was filled with smoke in the year 2 Acatl. Thus it came about
that we who are now living are here. The blaze started and was sus-
pended in the sky the year 1 Tochtli. The blaze started and fire
appeared because it had been night for twenty-five years. Thus fire
began in the sky in the year 1 Tochtli. After that the dogs made smoke,
as has been said. After the fire started, Tezcatlipoca started the fire,
with which the sky was smoked again in the year 2 Acatl.

In this part of the myth, we see how Titlacahuan, one of the gods
who was no other than the red Tezcatlipoca (also called Tlalclauque or
Tlatlauhqui), harbored a couple to whom he gave ears of corn for nourishment. We can see a similarity to the account about the couple in
which Cipactonal and Oxomoco were created and the elements the

gods gave them. It is interesting to see how this pair made fire and how it annoyed the gods, how Tezcatlipoca punished them by turning them into dogs and then created fire, which later would be so important to both humankind and to the gods. It seemed that the god wanted to create something new and useful to humankind.

Because Tezcatlipoca created and then destroyed the couple, Quetzalcoatl had a chance to try to create humans again. This is pointed out as the account continues.

III.   Creation of Humans

The gods talked to each other and said, "Who will live there, since the sky is set up and the Lord of the Earth has been set up. Who will live there, o gods?" The matter was taken up by Citlaliicue, Citlallatonac, Apanteuctli, Tepanquizqui, Tlallamanqui, Huictlolinqui, Quetzalcóhuatl, and Titlacahuan. Then Quetzalcóhuatl went to hell (Mictlan, among the dead). He approached Mictlanteuctli and Mictlancíhuatl and said to them, "I have come for the precious bones that you are guarding."

The latter answered, "What will you do with them, Quetzalcóhuatl?"

He replied, "The gods want to make the ones who will inhabit the earth from them."

Mictlanteuctli answered, "So be it. Play my conch horn and carry it around my throne of precious stones four times."

But the conch horn did not have any finger holes. He called the worms, and they made holes for him, and immediately bumblebees and wild bees came and played it, and Mictlanteuctli heard it. He spoke again, saying, "It is all right. Take them."

Then Mictlanteuctli said to his messengers, the Mixtec, "Go tell him, gods, that he has to leave them here."

But Quetzalcóhuatl called back to him, "No, I am going to take them forever." And he said to his *nahual* [animal alter ego], "Tell him that I will come to leave them." The *nahual* came, yelling, "I will come to leave them."

He climbed up quickly after he gathered the precious bones. The bones of a male were on one side, and the bones of a woman on the other side. Thus Quetzalcóhuatl took them, making a bundle that he carried off.

Mictlanteuctli again spoke to his messengers, "Gods, Quetzalcóhuatl has really taken the precious bones. Gods, hurry up and make a hole."

They hastened to do so. Quetzalcóhuatl fell into the hole, was bruised and frightened by quails. He fainted and scattered the precious bones on the ground. They were bitten and chewed by the quails. A short time afterward Quetzalcóhuatl revived, wept, and said to his *nahual,* "How can this be, my *nahual?*" The *nahual* answered, "Because it has to be. The affair is spoiled, it is lost."

Then he gathered up the bones, bound them together, and took them immediately to Tamoanchan. After he had brought them, the one called Quilaztli ground them up. She is Cihuacohuatl, and she put them into a precious vessel. Quetzalcóhuatl bled his penis over them, and all of the gods mentioned above—Apanteuctli, Huictlolinqui, Tepanquizqui, Tlallamanac, Tzontemoc, and the sixth one among them, Quetzalcóhuatl—did penance. Then they said, "The servants of the gods have been born." Because they did penance for us.

This is one of the most significant anthropogenic Nahua myths, the creation of humankind. Several things should be noted. One of them is the concern of the gods that someone inhabit the earth. This supports our previous argument that all of these myths were related to the central actor, humanity itself. There is something else of great importance: how Quetzalcoatl, whose mission it was to create the new age (sun) and humankind, went to Mictlan to gather the bones of their ancestors deposited there. It is important to stress, as we did on another occasion,[47] the presence of the elements of fertility on the one hand and those of sacrifice and death on the other, both of them employed to give humans life. We therefore believe that the conch horn that Mictlantecuhtli, lord of the place of the dead, owned was a fertility symbol. He asked Quetzalcoatl to play it and go around his precious seat four times,

47. Matos Moctezuma 1978c.

but the conch horn had no life; it had not been fertilized. Therefore it was necessary for the worms to perforate it and the bees to go inside it to give it sound. When he heard it, the god agreed to allow Quetzalcoatl to take the bones and carry them away, but shortly afterward he repented and placed obstacles in the latter's way. Quetzalcoatl fell down dead but later came to life and sought his *nahual.*

Finally, he took the bones to the place of the gods, Tamoanchan, where the sexual act took place. Quilaztli ground the bones and placed them in her vessel, and the god again sacrificed by drawing blood from his penis and mixing this divine semen with the bones of the dead in order to give life to humans, accomplished through the penance of the gods. Thus the *macehuales,* "the deserved through sacrifice," were born. The version given in the "Anales de Cuauhtitlan" states that Quetzalcoatl was searching for the place where his father's bones were buried, and once he had found them, he placed them, or buried them, in the "royal house called Quilaztli."

It is crucial here to indicate the role that the sacrifice of the gods, and of Quetzalcoatl himself, played in achieving life, an act that was repeated later when the sun that would give light to the new humans was created. It is also basic to understand the presence of opposing elements that imply duality: the dead element (bones) that will be revived by blood. Here we have the principle of the sacrifice that would be crucial in producing life. Quetzalcoatl had to bleed his penis, and the gods had to do penance. That created the first bargain between humans and the gods. Just as the latter had to make sacrifices so that humankind might live, so humans had to give their blood and repeat the sacrifice in order for the universe to continue and for the sun not to halt. It was also necessary for the gods to be sacrificed and to die in order for the new sun, the fifth, to emerge in Teotihuacan. Before that, once humans were created, the gods worried about their nourishment. And once again it was Quetzalcoatl who had the opportunity to obtain their sustenance.

IV.   Creation of Food

They spoke again, saying, "What will they eat, o gods? All of them are looking for food." Then the ant went into the Tonacatepetl (mountain of sustenance), and took a corn kernel. Quetzalcóhuatl met the ant and asked, "Where did you get that?" He asked him time and again, but it didn't want to tell him. At last it said, "There," pointing out the place, and it led him there. Quetzalcóhuatl became a black ant and went with it. They entered, and both of them carried it. Quetzalcóhuatl went with the red ant to the deposit, arranged the corn, and took it immediately to Tamoanchan. The gods chewed it and put it in our mouths to strengthen us. Then they said, "What will we do with the Tonacate-petl?" Quetzalcóhuatl went by himself, tied it up with cords, and tried to carry it on his back, but he couldn't lift it. Then Oxomoco cast lots with the corn, and Cipactonal, Oxomoco's wife, did the same, because Cipactonal is a woman. Then Oxomoco and Cipactonal said that only Nanahuatl ("the pimply one") could free Tonacatepetl's grain by pound-ing it with a stick, because they had divined it. The *tlaloques* (rain gods) — the blue *tlaloque,* the white *tlaloque,* the yellow *tlaloque,* and the red *tlaloque* — were summoned; Nanahuatl struck the grain off the cobs with his blows. Then the *tlaloques* snatched the food: the white, the black, the yellow, and the red corn; the beans; the amaranths; the chia; the fish amaranth. All the food was snatched away.[48]

This myth is fundamental to what we propose to demonstrate later.

It should be pointed out here that the food was found inside a hill called Tonacatepetl, which means "mountain of our sustenance." This is important because in Chapter 5 we will see how this hill was related to the Templo Mayor. But we also see the concern of the gods to provide food for humankind, obliging Quetzalcoatl to perform various acts to obtain it. Once again the gods intervened. Their participation was always necessary and can be understood as a kind of prefatory sanctifi-cation to validate what was being created.

The *tlaloques,* helpers of Tlaloc, the god of water, rain, and fertility, were prominently featured. The Tonacatepetl was thus linked to the gods of rain because the grain flourished only through them.

Up to this point we have had the earth, fire, humankind, and the grain to feed them, but the sun to illuminate the earth and give life to the plants was lacking. That creation took place in Teotihuacan.

---

48. This myth is important to our proposal that the Tlaloc side of the temple is a hill, as we mentioned in another article (Matos Moctezuma 1980).

V.   Creation of the Sun

The name of this sun was Nauh Ollin (Four Movement). This is our very own, belonging to those who are living today. This was its signal, the one that is here, because it fell into the sun's fire in the divine oven of Teotihuacan. It was the same sun of Topiltzin (our sun), of Tollan, and of Quetzalcóhuatl. Before becoming the sun, his name was Nanáhuatl, who was from Tamoanchan. Eagle, tiger, hawk, wolf; Chicuacén Ecatl (Five Wind), Chicuacén Xochitl (Six Flower)—both of these are names of the sun. What is here now is called Teotexcalli (Divine Oven) that burned for years. Tonacateuctli (Lord of Our Flesh) and Xiuhteuctli (Lord of the Year) called out to Nanáhuatl, saying, "Now you will watch over heaven and earth." He became very sad and said, "What are you gods saying? I am a poor, sickly being." They also summoned Nahui Técpatl, who is the moon. Tlalocanteuctli (Lord of Paradise) and Nappateuctli (Four Times Lord) called him. Then Nanáhuatl fasted. He took his thorns and his branches of wild laurel (*acxoyatl*) and arranged for the moon to be provided with thorns. First Nanáhuatl drew sacrificial blood from himself. Afterward the moon sacrificed: his laurel branches were rich plumes (*quetzalli*) and his thorns *chalchihuites* that gave off incense. After four days Nanahuatl was painted white and feathered. Then he jumped into the fire. Nahui Técpatl meanwhile sang and danced for him. Nanáhuatl jumped into the fire, and immediately afterward the moon jumped into the ashes. When he went, the eagle seized him and carried him off. The tiger couldn't take him but jumped over him and landed in the fire. That is why he is spotted. Afterward the hawk was smoked and then the wolf was scorched there. None of the three could carry him. In this way he arrived in the sky. As soon as he reached the sky, Tonacateuctli and Tonacacíhuatl honored him. They seated him on a throne of *quecholli* feathers and placed a crimson band around his head. He stayed in the sky for four days and came to a stop on the sign Nauh Ollin. He didn't move for four days; he was quiet.

The gods said to him, "Why don't you move?" Then they sent Itztlotli (the obsidian hawk), who went to the sun and questioned him, saying, "The gods are speaking and asking why you don't move." The sun replied, "Because I need their blood and their realm."

The gods consulted with each other, and Tlahuizcalpanteuctli, who was angry, said, "Why don't we shoot him with an arrow? If only he would move!" He shot at him but missed. Ah! Ah! The sun shot at Tlahuiz-calpanteuctli with his crimson feather arrows and right away covered his face with all of the nine heavens, because Tlahuizcalpanteuctli was ice. Then the gods Titlacahuan and Huitzilopochtli and the women Xochiquetzal, Yapaliicue, and Nochpaliicue met together and it was then that the death of the gods occurred, alas, in Teotihuacan.

When the sun went to the sky, the moon, who had only jumped into the ashes, also went, and he had barely reached the edge of the sky when Papáztac broke his face with a rabbit-shaped vessel. Afterward some spirits and some demons came to meet him at the crossroads, and they said to him, "You are welcome here."

When they stopped him, they put rags on his body. They came to give him that offering at the same time the sun stopped in the Nauh Ollin because it was late.

Here again we see the intervention of Quetzalcoatl. Other gods, such as Tonatecuhtli, who occupies the thirteenth heaven, and Xiuhtecuhtli, who was at the center of the universe, also participated. We again see the sacrifice of the gods, as in the case of Nanahuatzin and of the moon, who autosacrificed with thorns before casting themselves into the divine oven, the fire. Then the Fifth Sun emerged, rose, and was received by the firstborn pair. Above all else, it was necessary for the sun to move, and the gods sent the obsidian hawk to ask him why he didn't do so. The sun's reply was conclusive: a sacrifice by the gods was necessary. Once again the gods had to sacrifice themselves and die for humans because only in that way would the sun be able to move. It was a repetition of the gods' arrangement to give life through sacrifice.

Sahagún gave us similar version of this cosmogonic myth, in which Nanahuatzin and Tecuciztecatl took part. [49] The first one was converted into the sun, and the second became the moon. In this version it is important to point out that it was Quetzalcoatl who knew in what direction the sun would rise, since some gods expected to see it rise in the

49. Sahagún 1956.

north and some in other directions of the universe. Only Quetzalcoatl and Totec looked toward the east, where it finally emerged. This is worth noting because, as part of their cosmovision, it was related to the placement of the buildings in the sacred precinct of Tenochtitlan.

A review of the myths just cited will clear up several matters. Although a thorough analysis of their various versions is needed, we can obtain interesting data that will allow us to understand some of the beliefs and explanations of Nahua cosmovision.

First, all of these myths have an internal order explaining how an age, or a sun, emerged. They begin by relating a cosmogonic and an anthropogenic myth, about the creation of the time before humans and the creation of human food. In each age, or sun, this was a constant element. Humans, in whatever age, could not exist without their corresponding nourishment. Here we see the real need for the survival of humankind: food and all that it implies.

Another constant is the creation-destruction taking place in each age. The conflict of the gods (Tezcatlipoca and Quetzalcoatl) was what impelled the process, a constant cycle of creation (life) and destruction (death). We could interpret that cosmic combat or struggle as the desire of each god for the sun he created (and a sun would include the kind of humans and their corresponding food, etc.) to survive on the earth, something the other god could not allow and would endeavor to destroy. In this alternation the creation of the Fifth Sun corresponded to Quetzalcoatl, and it in turn would be destroyed by Tezcatlipoca. We see in the "Anales de Cuauhtitlan" that this happened through earthquakes. The "Anales" state, "According to what the elders have said, because it moved, walked, in the Fifth Sun, sign of the (movement) called Ollin Tonatiuh (Sun of Movement), there will be earthquakes and general starvation of which we will perish."[50]

We do not agree entirely with León Portilla's[51] argument that the humans of the Fifth Sun, the Mexica, tried to preserve the universal order and to avoid the final cataclysm by resorting to warfare and sacrifice as a

---

[50] "Anales de Cuauhtitlan" in *Códice Chimalpopoca* 1945.
[51] León Portilla 1963: 36–37.

part of their attempt to maintain and to prolong the vital energy of the Fifth Sun. Rather, we think their actions were intended to continue the course of the sun to which they belonged, not to avoid the fate of the previous suns, that is, their destruction. We believe they thought that through the constant struggle between the gods, the Fifth Sun and its humans, like the preceding suns, would also disappear by the movement of the earth. That concept explains the fire that was renewed every fifty-two years on the Cerro de la Estrella for fear that the sun might not rise the following morning, that the dreaded moment of destruction and change had arrived. Sahagún, referring to that ritual, stated,

> When that night came when the new fire had to be lit and spread, everyone was terrified and fearfully waited for what might happen, for they had this fable or belief among them that if fire could not be made, it would be the end of the human race and night and those shadows would be eternal, and that the sun would not again be born or rise, and that from on high would come down and descend on them the *tzitzimime,* terrible and ugly beings who would devour men and women.[52]

A terrible uncertainty and anguish in confronting life and death can be clearly seen in Nahua poems.[53]

The "Leyenda de los soles," which tells about the creation of the Fifth Sun, is useful to us in presenting the sequence followed by the corresponding god for the creation of the new sun: (a) the founding of the earth; (b) the creation of a human couple; (c) the creation of fire; (d) the creation of humans; (e) the creation of the new sun.

All these steps have to be evaluated in the light of the gods' intervention. Fire could not be made by a human couple; it had to be created by a god. Humans were in turn created by a mixture of blood and bones, but the death or sacrifice of the gods was indispensable. The sun, which had remained stationary, depended on the penance of the gods in order to move. From this we see another important aspect: the constant presence of the sacrifice of the gods in these myths. Without

---

[52.] Sahagún 1956.

[53.] In Appendix 2 we have included several Nahua poems that clearly express that anguish.

that act, nothing attained life or movement. In other words, every creative act had to be preceded by the sacrifice or death of a deity. Thus death and life were converted into cause and effect, one leading to the other, as we have seen in the acts of Tezcatlipoca and Quetzalcoatl.

We wish to point out, however, that all these perfectly concatenated myths had at their fundamental center humanity and the way it was sustained on earth. The gods were concerned with humanity's existence on earth, and to this end they directed all their efforts, including their self-sacrifice. According to Alfonso Caso,[54] that was so because the gods needed someone to feed them, to become their collaborator, because if that did not take place, they would perish as well. We do not agree with this statement because, according to the myths, the gods existed before the creation of humans. Therefore they did not need to be fed. What was necessary was that the universal order be maintained and that the cycles continue. Humans had to nourish only the sun and the earth to which they belonged until the gods decided upon their destruction so that they might create a new sun. The gods would die only in order to create humankind once again.

From the above, we can see how important sacrifice was among the Mexica. On the one hand an effort was made to repeat the sacrifice and death of the gods, and in many cases the sacrifice acquired the characteristics of the god to whom it was offered. On the other hand the purpose was to guarantee that the sun would not stop, that it would continue its march, which had begun, according to myth, by the sacrifice of the gods. During the ritual of sacrifice, humans continued to sacrifice gods. Death served as the germ of life.

One of the most important conclusions to be drawn from the above is that the Mexica, as humans of the Fifth Sun, belonged to that sun, or age, and would make sacrifices to the gods in the person of captives, slaves, other members of the society, so that the sun, born in Teotihuacan, would not stop its course. The gods had to continue to die, as was shown in the myth, in order for the universe to continue. A man, converted into a god at the moment of sacrifice, performed what the god did *in illo tempore*. Death was the means of obtaining life. But the

---

[54.] Caso 1958.

humans of that sun knew that some day, when Tezcatlipoca confronted Quetzalcoatl, they would disappear, just as had occurred in other ages. In reality each sun was in itself a totality that would be destroyed to give way to another. The Mexica moved within that dialectic, and their anguish over disappearing through the action of the gods led them to have serious doubts about their existence and about the afterworld. Because of this (fatalistic?) attitude, every fifty-two years they hoped to live on earth a little longer, but they were aware that sooner or later they would cease to exist. This explains another aspect that has been discussed for a century: what happens to the dead that go to Mictlan? According to Chavero,[55] there is a materialistic principle at work here because after four years the individual disappears completely. We believe that what happens can be explained if we understand the mode of thought we are analyzing. The dead do not go on to other suns; only their bones are deposited in Mictlan, as the prior anthronecrogenic myth revealed. We believe that this fate included the warrior killed in battle or sacrifice, who was transformed into a bird with beautiful plumage or into a butterfly. He would endure as long as the sun whom he accompanied also survived. Thereafter everything would disappear.

It should be pointed out that this kind of thinking derived from humans' observation of everything around them: people, plants, animals, the day. Everything is born and dies, a cycle that is constantly repeated. It is the only way the universe and its renewal can be conceptualized. The refrain "One lives only once on earth" expresses this in poetry. Everything has to go through the cycle, so there is no belief that people or the sun to which they belong will endure. That would break the pattern of everything created. What has to be maintained is the constant cycle, the eternal, inevitable struggle between Tezcatlipoca and Quetzalcoatl.

Myth of Huitzilopochtli's Birth and Struggle

From the preceding myths we want to highlight the one that tells of the search for food by Quetzalcoatl on the Tonacatepetl, as that myth, which we now tell according to Sahagún, refers to another hill where

---

55. Chavero 1887.

the solar god Huitzilopochtli was born. The existence of these hills in their corresponding myths will be indispensable to our later argument in regard to the Templo Mayor. The theogonic myth of the birth and struggle of Huitzilopochtli is essential. It is an example of what we mentioned earlier, a myth that emerges from a real historical event. It is necessary to go back to the time of the pilgrimage of the Mexica in order to find data in both Durán[56] and Tezozomoc[57] about an important event that took place when the group settled in Coatepec (Hill of the Serpent) near Tula.

According to those chroniclers, a group, or barrio, the Huitznahua, who had come from Aztlan as part of the larger group, decided to remain there. Huitzilopochtli's followers objected, and the god became angry and decided to destroy the Huitznahua during the night. This rebellion, which was headed by Coyolxauhqui, was put down, assuring the dominance of Huitzilopochtli's followers.

Durán tells that the Mexica, among them the Huitznahua, left Aztlan in seven groups. This historical event that Yolotl González Torres correctly interpreted as an internal struggle for power gave rise to a myth in which the conflict among humans became a struggle among the gods. Before continuing, let us see what the mythologized historical event tells us.

> At Coatepec, near Tula, there dwelt one day, there lived a woman named Coatl icue, mother of the Centzonuitznaua. And their elder sister was named Coyolxauhqui.

> And this Coatl icue used to perform penances there; she used to sweep; she used to take care of the sweeping. Thus she used to perform penances at Coatepec. And once, when Coatl icue was sweeping, feathers descended upon her—what was like a ball of feathers. Then Coatl icue snatched them up; she placed them at her waist. And when she had swept, then she would have taken the feathers which she had put at her waist. She found nothing. Thereupon by means of them Coatl icue conceived.

[56.] Durán 1967. Yolotl González Torres (1958) has given an interpretation of the combat that was going to take place between the two groups. However, we don't think it contradicts what Seler said about the myth.

[57.] Tezozomoc 1975.

Huitzilopochtli in battle gear atop the temple-hill, (*Códice Azcatitlan*).

And when the Centzonuitznaua saw that their mother was already with child, they were very wrathful. They said: "Who brought this about? Who got her with child? She hath dishonored us; she hath shamed us."

And their elder sister, Coyolxauhqui, said to them: "My elder brothers, she hath dishonored us. We [can] only kill our mother, the wicked one who is already with child. Who is the cause of what is in her womb?"

And when Coatl icue learned of this, she was sorely afraid, she was deeply saddened. But her child, who was in her womb, comforted her; he called to her; he said to her: "Have no fear. Already I know [what I shall do]."

When Coatl icue heard the words of her child, she was much comforted by them; she was satisfied [concerning] what had thus terrified her.

And upon this the Centzonuitznaua, when they had brought together all their considerations, when they had expressed their determination that they would kill their mother, because she had brought about an affront, much exerted themselves. They were very wrathful. As if her heart came forth, Coyolxauhqui greatly incited, aroused the anger of her elder brothers, that they would kill their mother. And the Centzonuitznaua thereupon arrayed themselves; they armed themselves for war.

And these Centzonuitznaua were like seasoned warriors. They twisted their hair; they wound their hair about their heads; they wound about their heads their hair, their forehead hair.

But one who was named Quauitl icac delivered information to both sides. That which the Centzonuitznaua said he then told, he informed Uitzilopochtli.

And Uitzilopochtli said to Quauitl icac: "Pay careful heed, my dear uncle; listen carefully. I already know [what I shall do]."

And upon this, when finally [the Centzonuitznaua] expressed their determination, when they were of one mind in their deliberations, that they would kill, that they would slay their mother, thereupon they went. Coyolxauhqui led them. Much did each one exert himself; each one persevered; each one armed himself for war. Each one was provided. On them[selves] they placed their paper array, the paper crowns, their nettles hanging from the painted papers; and they bound little bells to the calves of their legs. These little bells were called *oyohualli*. And their arrows had notched heads.

Thereupon they went. They went each one in order. They went each one in his row. Each one wielded his weapons. They went crouching. Coyolxauhqui led them.

And Quauitl icac thereupon ran up [the hill] to warn Uitzilopochtli. He said to him: "Already they are coming."

Then Uitzilopochtli said: "Watch well where they come."

Thereupon Quauitl icac said to him: "Already they are at Tzompantitlan."

Again Uitzilopochtli spoke forth to him: "Where now do they come?"

Then [Quauitl icac] said to him: "Already they are at Coaxalpan."

Once more Uitzilopochtli spoke forth to Quauitl icac: "See where they now come."

Then [this one] said to him: "Already they are at Apetlac."

Once again [Uitzilopochtli] spoke forth to him: "Where now do they come?"

Then Quauitl icac said to him: "Already they come along the slope."

And Uitzilopochtli again spoke forth to Quauitl icac: he said to him: "Watch where they now come."

Then Quauitl icac said to him: "At last they scale the heights here; at last they arrive here. Coyolxauhqui cometh leading them."

And Uitzilopochtli just then was born.

Then he had his array with him—his shield, *teueuelli*; and his darts and his blue dart thrower, called *xiuatlatl*; and in diagonal stripes was his face painted with his child's offal, called his child's face painting. He was pasted with feathers at his forehead and at his ears. And on his one thin foot, his left, he had the sole pasted with feathers. And he had stripes in blue mineral earth on both his thighs and both his upper arms.

And one named Tochancalqui set fire to the [serpent] *xiuhcoatl*. Uitzilopochtli commanded it.

Then he pierced Coyolxauhqui, and then he quickly struck off her head. It stopped there at the edge of Coatepetl. And her body came falling below; it fell breaking to pieces; in various places her arms, her legs, her body fell.

And Uitzilopochtli then arose; he pursued, gave full attention to the Centzonuitznaua; he plunged, he scattered them from the top of the Coatepetl.

And when he had come driving them to the ground below, thereupon he took after them; he pursued all of them around Coatepetl. Four times he chased them all around, pursued them all around. Yet in vain they went crying out at him, yet in vain they cried out against him, yet in vain they went striking their shields. No more could they do, no more could they achieve; no longer could they ward him off. Uitzilopochtli just set on all of them; he indeed made them turn tail; he indeed destroyed them; he indeed annihilated them; he indeed exterminated them.

And when even now he indeed did not leave them alone, when indeed he hung on to all of them, much did they importune him. They said to him: "Let this be enough!"

But Uitzilopochtli did not content himself with this. He was very bold against them as he took after them. And only very few fled his presence. Those who escaped his hands went there to the south. For indeed toward there these Centzonuitznaua went, the few who escaped the hands of Uitzilopochtli.

And upon this, when he had slain them, when he had taken his pleasure, he took from them their goods, their adornment, the paper crown. He took them as his own goods, he took them as his own property; he assumed them as his due, as if taking the insignia to himself.

And Uitzilopochtli was called an omen of evil, because only from a feather which fell, his mother Coatl icue conceived. For no one appeared as his father.

This one the Mexicans respected. Hence they made offerings to him; hence they honored him, they exerted themselves for him. And they placed their trust in Uitzilopochtli. And this veneration was taken from there, Coatepec, as was done in days of yore.[58]

The first thing we will call attention to in this myth is the place where it took place, Coatepec, near Tula. We believe the Mexica paid tribute to the Toltecs from the time they arrived in Aztlan and that internal disputes in Tula weakened the Toltecs, making it possible for some of the tributary groups, such as the Mexica, to move to the center and contribute to the destruction of the Toltec city. This sequence was repeated by the Mexica some years later with their oppressor in Azcapotzalco, and perhaps something similar occurred in Teotihuacan. What is certain is that they settled in Coatepec and from there went to Tula around A.D. 1156 or 1165, a year that coincides with the destruction of that city. However that may be, it is evident that there was a connection between the birth of Huitzilopochtli, their war god, and a subsequent attack on Tula. Perhaps the differences between the districts, which gave victory to Huitzilopochtli over Coyolxauhqui and reinforced his power, had begun before the attack. The Coatepec-Tula connection leads us to believe that besides an internal struggle for power, a battle took place against the Toltec oppressor. In brief, there is no doubt that the Mexica engaged in transcendent battles, which was the reason their chief god was born to fight and the hill of Coatepec was the location of that combat.

Coatepec, then, is a place of the gods. Coatlicue, mother of the gods and of earth, a goddess doing penance while sweeping, was there. It is interesting that the broom became her symbol in her various avatars, for example, Toci. A relevant aspect of the myth was the pregnancy of the goddess through a feather she found and placed in her bosom. It should be recalled that a young Mexican girl who became pregnant was said to have a precious feather inside her. That angered the Centzonhuitznahua, the innumerable southerners, who were incited by their sister Coyolxauhqui to kill their mother for dishonoring them. We do not doubt that the interpretation given by Seler and accepted by various scholars is correct. Here a real, historical combat was utilized by humans to explain the daily struggle between the sun and the nocturnal forces. These two

---

[58] Sahagún 1950–1970, bk. 3: 1–5.

interpretations were not exclusive. The sun emerges from the earth from the east; it is her son. We know that the myth's reference to the 400 southerners and the statement that they moved southward was also a reference to the stars in that part of the sky because that was their name. The role of Quauitl icac, the southerner who helped Huitzilopochtli, is important. He told the sun about the movement of the stars. His name means "eagle that is on foot," or "steadfast."

Coyolxauhqui is the moon. That is clear from the way she is depicted in the best-known versions, in addition to the very significant dismemberment of her body that can be seen in the sculpture at the Templo Mayor. In other societies such dismemberment is related to the lunar phases because, unlike the sun, the moon suffers mutilations (the quarter moon, the waning of the moon, etc.). It is identified with what is feminine, also a lunar characteristic. Therefore it made sense that the battle take place at night and that the stars were scattered throughout the sky so that the sun could emerge triumphant from the east. We should not dismiss the idea that the myth signaled the replacement of the lunar calendar by the solar calendar, but that would require further study.

We should comment on something that is immediately obvious. Huitzilopochtli, as a god, was the one who ordered the Mexica to leave Aztlan. The god existed before his birth in Coatepec. However, what occurred in that place was of such magnitude (the strengthening of internal power and freedom from the Toltecs) that it was necessary to endow the birth of the god with a definite purpose—he was born to fight and to destroy the enemy.

It was a way of theologically justifying the warlike destiny of the Mexica. This destiny was the triumph of the sun, of day over night, and the need to feed the sun with the blood of warriors. The sun was a warrior and had to be nourished with the precious liquid of warriors. The importance of war was manifest in the link between Huitzilopochtli—sun who was born to fight the enemy—and the Mexica need for war to survive. Thus there were two elements that sustained the very existence of the Mexica: war, a means of taking possession through tribute of the products of the conquered groups, and water, a life-giving element that provided life to the plants. That is how the hills of Coatepec and its relationship to war and Tonacatepetl as a depository for food became the essential expression of the primordial needs of the Mexica.

5

And Humans Created the Templo

The survey we made of the principal Nahua myths now allows us to combine them with our central postulate that the Templo Mayor was the sacred place par excellence where several of these myths were presented and reenacted, so that the Templo was the locus of "living" myths. Moreover, it was the place where the vertical and the horizontal planes intersected, from which one could enter the celestial levels or the underworld. It was the center of the four directions of the universe, making it the navel and the fundamental center of Mexica cosmovision. It signified the nucleus of universal order, and the architecture of the edifice itself is a compendium of the above. In this way the Templo Mayor was endowed with significance and acquired the highest degree of sacrality.

Let us begin this chapter with the Temple itself. We begin with an analysis of the foundation of Tenochtitlan, how the sacred and profane spaces were separated, and how the fundamental center that the Templo would occupy was established. Next we see the significance of the Templo Mayor and its sacred precinct, with the Templo as a repository of the principal myths. We end with an account of how all this fits into our categories of phenomenon and essence.

The Founding of Tenochtitlan

Several sources, such as Durán and Tezozomoc, tell us that the first thing the Mexica would do upon arriving at various points on a pilgrimage was to erect a shrine to their god Huitzilopochtli. This would also occur when they reached the spot reserved for them, a place identified by certain signs that the god, through the priests, communicated to them. Regarding this, Durán said,

> The first thing they found was an entirely white, very beautiful juniper, at the foot of which a fountain flowed. The first thing they saw were the willows around the fountain, all of them white, without a single green leaf. All of the reeds as well as the cattails at the place were white. Frogs, also white, began to leap out of the water, and among them were some water snakes, all white and showy. The water emerged from two large stones so clear and beautiful it brought them great satisfaction.

Later, referring to other signs, he said, "Going from one place to another, they saw a prickly pear cactus, and on top of it, the eagle with its wings outspread to the sun's rays, enjoying the warmth and freshness of the morning. In its claws it held an elegant bird with precious and resplendent feathers."[59]

We have divided these omens into two. The first omen (the white color) was the same sign the Toltecs saw in Cholula, as told in the *Historia Tolteca-Chichimeca,* and the Mexica must have borrowed the omen from them. In contrast, the second omen, which tells of the eagle perched on a cactus devouring birds or serpents, might very well have been truly Mexica and could have symbolized the triumph of the sun (eagle) of Huitzilopochtli over his enemies. It is evident that the Mexica borrowed many elements, mythical as well as others, from their predecessors, incorporating them into their own tradition, as was the case with the ideas of the seven tribes, Chicomoztoc, Colhuacatepetl, and others. Their own omens derived from certain events that were significant to them and that then became mythical. We know that when the Mexica arrived, the center of Mexico was occupied by several groups who allowed the Mexica to settle in their territory on the condition

---

[59.] Durán 1967.

Chicomoztoc-Colhuacatepec according to the *Historia Tolteca-Chichimeca*.

(characteristic of all Mesoamerica) that they pay tribute and help in their wars. This was the case in Azcapotzalco, where they were allowed to occupy the islands in the lake. This meant that they did not settle where they chose but where the people who had control of those lands allowed them to stay. However, it was important for the Mexica and for people in general to have, or to create, the signs that indicated their supposed relationship to the gods and their status as a chosen people.

When they settled on the island, the first thing they did was to construct a shrine to their god at the place where the eagle had supposedly been found, in order to mark off the four quarters that had as their center the temple itself. Writing about this, Durán said,

> The following night the Mexicans erected a shrine where their god was, having filled most of the lagoon and having prepared the wood and the foundations to make their houses. Huitzilopochtli spoke to his priest or guardian, saying, "Tell the Mexican congregation to divide themselves into four principal districts—each with its lord, his relatives, friends, and partisans—placing in the center the house you have built for my repose, and let each group build its district as it pleases.[60]

One of the clearest representations of that event is Plate 1 of the Códice Mendoza, in the center of which can be seen the eagle and under it the name of Tenochtitlan. Around it are the four areas where the four major districts were established corresponding to the four directions of the universe, that is, the horizontal plane. The place where the eagle was found became the site for the Templo Mayor.

With the construction of the temple at the center, sacred space was separated from the profane. The former included the ceremonial precinct that contained the other temples (seventy-eight of them, according to Sahagún) with very precise boundaries. The latter was the civil area that corresponded to dwelling places and districts, or *calpulli*. The Templo Mayor was the fundamental center, the place where the principal omen had been discovered, as told by the chronicles. At the same time, it was the point from which begin the four quarters that in turn imply the four directions of the universe.

Mircea Eliade's studies of various religions point out that each new settlement or founding of a city is accompanied by omens and that sacred space generally becomes a defined area that becomes an

---

[60.] Durán 1967.

"inexhaustible fountain" of sacrality. The place is always "discovered" by humans through certain omens filled with hierophany, among which an animal is often present. There is an amazing similarity in the symbolic use of the four quarters to represent the universe in different religions. Referring to this, Eliade continued, "The founding of a new town repeats the creation of the world; once the spot has been confirmed by ritual, a square or circular enclosure is put round it with four gates corresponding to the four points of the compass. . . . Towns are divided into four in imitation of the Cosmos; in other words, they are a copy of the Universe."[61] This may be the answer to the archaeologist's question why buildings were superimposed, never changing their location: they continued to occupy the sacred space and to establish the fundamental center.

Symbolism of the Templo Mayor and the Ceremonial Precinct

The Templo Mayor was thus converted into the fundamental center where all the sacred power was found and all the levels intersected. We believe, however, that it not only occupied that privileged place but that the very form and characteristics of its architecture represented all of the Mexica cosmogonic concepts. Let us look at this more closely.

Through the archaeological data we have been able to obtain during our work at the Templo Mayor (as well as the information from historical sources such as Sahagún, Durán, etc., to which we have referred in other works[62]), we know that the Templo Mayor was an edifice that rested upon a general platform, to which one climbed from the great plaza, or ceremonial precinct, by a single stairway with only a few steps. A series of serpents was on the platform. Two of them have undulating bodies, and on their great heads traces of the original color that covered them can still be found. Both are at the north and south ends of the platform where some chambers are, and their heads and bodies are oriented toward those cardinal points—that is, the one on the north end

---

61. Eliade 1958: 374.
62. Matos Moctezuma 1981.

faces south, and vice versa. In other words they are facing each other, but at a great distance. In the exact center there is the single serpent head, facing west, the direction toward which all of the Templo Mayor is oriented. Upon that great platform stood the enormous base of the Templo, with its principal characteristic, the two staircases that led to the upper part. On the balustrades of the two staircases are four serpent heads, two in the center marking the union of the two stairs and one at either end. The serpents are not alike. There is a difference in their elements. For example, the two on Huitzilopochtli's side have four nostrils. The others, on Tlaloc's side, have a kind of circle on their heads. On Huitzilopochtli's side, on the platform and near the middle of the stairs, the enormous Coyolxauhqui sculpture is found.

On the upper part the stairs lead to the place where two shrines are found, one to the god of water and the other to the god of war. In front of the latter is a sacrificial stone, while at the front of the entrance to the other is a polychrome *chac-mool*. Although these last elements appeared in one of the first building stages of the Templo Mayor, we believe that they must have been repeated in the following expansions of the building because they are elements that belong to a number of concepts linked to the Templo itself. Then, too, several chroniclers tell about the location of the sacrificial stone, and their accounts correspond exactly to what we found in our excavations.

From the description above and following our study, we find that the building itself represented the cosmovision of the Mexica. We believe that the platform where the serpents are located represented the terrestrial level, that is, the horizontal plane. Apart from the significance of the serpent as a terrestrial element, the greatest number of offerings were found below the floor of this platform. Another interesting fact is that above the platform and all around the Templo great braziers were found on both sides of the serpent heads. These groupings were located in the middle of the north and south facades as well as at the rear facade (east), and at the center of each one of the Tlaloc and Huitzilopochtli structures. This proves that the platform was where people made offerings to the gods. The remains of a small stairway leading to the platform was found in the rear facade. This surely was for the purpose of lighting the braziers. Such stairs were not found in other parts of the base, which might mean that the upper parts of the platform where the shrines to the principal gods were located symbolized the celestial levels, the place where the dual deity resided, the Omeyocan.

As to the lower levels, these go from the Templo platform (earthly level) downward. The two parts composing the Templo Mayor represented two sacred hills or mountains, Huitzilopochtli's, the hill of Coatepec, and Tlaloc's, Tonacatepetl, Mountain of Our Sustenance. What is interesting is that the two hills collectively may represent the first step to Mictlan, the two hills that collide. Sahagún wrote, "You will see here that you have to pass between the two mountains that clash, one with the other. . . ."[63]

This may explain why one of the two death sculptures in the offerings was found in offering 20, located at the back of the union of the two buildings. This is a vase that has a skeleton on one side. The other similar piece was found in offering 6, on Huitzilopochtli's side next to the sculpture of Coyolxauhqui.

The concept that the Templo Mayor itself represents the order of the universe and that it is the place, or center, where all the levels intersect (which we call the fundamental center) can also be seen in the principal temples of other religions. Eliade put it this way: "All of these sacred constructions represent the whole universe in symbol: their various floors or terraces are identified with the 'heavens' or levels of the Cosmos. In one sense, every one of them reproduces the cosmic mountain, is, in other words, held to be built at the 'centre of the world.' "[64] Later he added, "Indeed, by the very fact of being placed at the centre of the Cosmos, the temple or sacred city is always a meeting place for the three cosmic regions."[65]

In regard to the above, the words of the king of Texcoco, spoken to Ahuizotl at the feast celebrating the termination of one stage of the Templo Mayor, are interesting: "Therefore, since you are, though very young, the king of such a powerful realm, which is the root, the navel, and the heart of all this worldly mechanism, make sure that Mexican honor will

---

[63] Sahagún 1956.
[64] Eliade 1958: 373.
[65] Eliade 1958: 376.

not diminish but become even greater."[66] Yet the ceremonial precinct, with its seventy-eight buildings of which Sahagún spoke, was also closely tied to their cosmovision. The location of a building was not due to chance but had a reason related to the fundamental center, the Templo Mayor. Thus, according to the chroniclers, Ehecatl-Quetzalcoatl's building was located in front of the Templo Mayor. It was found in that location in Tlatelolco, a city contemporaneous with Tenochtitlan. Its principal facade faced east, possibly related to the Nahua myth about the creation of the sun in Teotihuacan, in which the gods awaited the rising of the sun and were looking in different directions. Ehecatl looked toward the east, and of course that is where the sun did rise. Durán mentioned this in referring to the distribution of some of the buildings at the ceremonial precinct:

> The four main temples had entrances facing toward those directions, and the four gods that were in them. Their faces were turned toward the same directions. The reason for this, although it was not a fable, should be told in order to clear up the mystery.

> The ancient ones believed that before the sun came up, even before it was created, the gods had a big debate, arguing about where it would be convenient for the sun to come up and that this should be determined before they created it. Each one wanted it to come out his way. One of them said that it was very necessary for it to come from the north; another said not so, that it was better for it to come from the south; still another said that it should arise in the west; and the other that it would be more convenient for it to come from the east. The latter had his wish come true, and he was facing in the direction where the sun arose. The others faced toward the directions they had chosen. For that reason there are four doors. . . .[67]

The location of some of the temples unearthed during the Templo Mayor Project was also interesting. While excavating the patio on the northern side, we found three shrines, designated with letters, a few meters apart along the northern facade of the Templo. Shrine A is oriented

[66.] Durán 1967.
[67.] Durán 1967.

from east to west and has two stairs that lead to the upper part. One faces west, and the other east. Building B (the one in the center) has a stairway to the west and is decorated on three sides with more than 240 stucco-covered stone skulls. The third edifice, C, is completely painted, with its principal facade facing the east. A building similar to this one is located on the other side of the Templo Mayor, on the southern side, and at the same height as the first. This led us to believe that if we excavated some more on the southern side, we would find shrines similar to A and B, but it was not so. Our error was to rely on an aesthetic hypothesis, assuming that many pre-Hispanic cultures used an axial symmetry — in other words, if an element were placed on one side, it would also be placed on the other to create an aesthetic equilibrium. If we had followed the hypothesis of the cosmovision that we now use, we would not have been misled, since there was no reason for an edifice on the southern side to be equivalent to the one with skulls found on the northern side. The latter had a specific symbolism according to Mexica cosmovision; it was the direction of Mictlampa, the region of the dead. Had we known that, our hypothesis would have been different, letting us see that there was no reason to have an edifice on the south side with the same characteristics, even though everything pointed to it based on aesthetics. We should have started from the hypothesis that to the Mexica what was most important about the ceremonial precinct, their sacred space, was to reproduce their own vision of the cosmos.

We will not go further into this topic, but we wish to clarify one important point. When we speak of the fundamental center, or the principal center, we are referring to the Templo Mayor. We say this because many centers exist, such as the ceremonial precinct as a whole or the city of Tenochtitlan; even an offering has its center, as do the houses or the temples of the *calpulli*. However, the Templo Mayor was the most important center, and we thus refer to it as the fundamental center.

The Templo Mayor as a Living Myth

Here we try to explain how the Templo Mayor, besides being the fundamental center of all the universe, was the place where some of the principal Nahua myths were reified and in some cases was itself a living myth, reenacted through ritual, with all its essential content.

The first point is that the Templo Mayor represented two mountains, Coatepec (Huitzilopochtli's side) and Tonacatepetl, or the Mountain of Sustenance (Tlaloc's side). The former has been pointed out by other writers, such as Paso y Troncoso in 1898 and, more recently, León Portilla in 1978. It is worthwhile, however, to add some facts on the matter that we have recently discovered. For instance, the Templo Mayor on Huitzilopochtli's side (the southern side) has some characteristics that have to do with the myth of his birth and the struggle between Huitzilopochtli and Coyolxauhqui on Coatepec. We have archaeological evidence of this, as well as information from written sources. Let us examine the first of the two:

1. The gods are located according to the myth. Both Huitzilopochtli and Coyolxauhqui had a specific position. The presence of Coyolxauhqui at the foot of the stairs proves that no object was placed randomly or just for decoration. The sculptures as well as the offerings all mean something because each object was placed in order to signify something. In the case of the goddess, she was found on the platform, on the terrestrial level, where she was hurled by her conquering brother, since the highest part of the hill is occupied by Huitzilopochtli.
2. Coyolxauhqui was depicted as decapitated and dismembered. This agrees with the mythical account that tells how she was beheaded and her body hurled down, becoming dismembered. The decapitation and the dismemberment were also related to the lunar phases and to femininity.
3. Huitzilopochtli, the conqueror, remained at the top of the hill-temple in his shrine, the walls and the benches of which have been found. Apparently the sculpture of Coatlicue (Toci), the mother goddess, was also at the top of the Templo.
4. On the last step of building stage II there is a face that might be of Quauitl icac, the one who told Huitzilopochtli where his brothers were advancing, or it might be that of Painal, although there are references that the latter might have been inside the shrine.

5. There is a sacrificial stone, the place of immolation, where Huitzilopochtli's treatment of Coyolxauhqui was repeated.
6. Coyolxauhqui was found in various building stages. At stage IVb there is a large sculpture of the goddess. There is another one just below that, at stage IV. There is also a stone fragment with part of the face of another Coyolxauhqui, similar to the first one, that might be from a later stage. We know that the diorite head of Coyolxauhqui comes from that area, but we do not know its exact location. This shows that her presence was repeated in the different enlargements of the Templo.
7. The representations of serpents in the Templo Mayor remind us of the name Coatepec, "hill of the serpent."
8. In the different sections of stage III, on Huitzilopochtli's side, are a series of protruding uncarved rocks that might be an attempt to give to the structure the appearance of a hill on his side, since there are none on Tlaloc's side.
9. We have suggested that perhaps some of the sculptures reclining on the stairway at this same stage III might represent the Centzonhuiznahua.
10. Decapitated female skulls were found in offerings to the goddess, which again reminds us of possible rituals in which a woman was sacrificed (beheading was associated principally with female sacrifices), in this case to reenact the myth.

The chronicles and codices also provide evidence of the hill-temple relationship. For example:

1. The description of the feast of Panquetzaliztli. Apart from the myth itself, it is one of the clearest pieces of evidence given in the chronicles. The feast was dedicated to Huitzilopochtli, and there are several aspects that are worth discussing.

   a. There is a journey of the slaves who were to die, carrying the mantles and *huipiles* [shifts] they were going to deposit in the Calpulco. This might be an evocation of the journey to reach Coatepec.

b. The sacrifice of four captives at the ball game (Tezozomoc) and elsewhere.

c. There was a skirmish between two groups of slaves. One group consisted of the Huitznahua, helped by the people from that colony.

d. The captives circled about the Templo, just as Huitzilopochtli was said to have pursued them around Coatepec.

e. The descent of Xiuhcoatl (fire serpent) imitated with torches and a paper head and tail in the form of a serpent. From its jaws red feathers emerged that seemed to represent flames.

f. After the captives and slaves were killed, the bodies were thrown down the staircases of the Templo, just as the god had cast Coyolxauhqui from the top of the hill, tearing her apart.

We believe that the custom of throwing down the bodies once they had been sacrificed mimics what Huitzilopochtli did to Coyolxauhqui in the myth. The dismemberment of the body at the bottom might also be a reenactment of the myth.

However, there was another ritual that alluded to the myth. In the month of Toxcatl, dedicated to Tezcatlipoca, an image of Huitzilopochtli was made out of amaranth dough (*tzoalli*) and placed in the Huitznahuac Temple, as Sahagún recorded:

> A platform on which to place the image was built in the temple called Huitznahuac. In it they used logs carved to look like serpents, whose heads were on the four sides of the platform, opposite to each other, so that all four sides had heads and tails. For making the image they used mesquite sticks for bones. Then they fattened it up with dough until they had shaped it in human form. They did this in the house where they always kept the image of Huitzilopochtli.
>
> After doing that they dressed it in all the trappings of Huitzilopochtli. . . .[68]

[68.] Sahagún 1956.

In his description of how they covered the figure, we see something very significant — the mantle was decorated with the image of a dismembered person (Coyolxauhqui?): "Underneath it they put some bones made of *tzoalli* near the feet of the image and covered them with the same mantle that covered everything, on which they had embroidered the bones and extremities of a dismembered person. The mantle, decorated in that way, was called *tlacuacuallo*."[69] Moreover, Sahagún told about how they sacrificed captives made to represent the Centzonhuitznahua gods in their temple: "The nineteenth edifice was called the Huitznahua teocalli. In it were placed the images of the gods called Centzonhuitznaua, in honor of Huitzilopochtli; and they sacrificed many captives. This was done each year at the feast of Panquetzaliztli."[70]

2. The description of the feast of Toci (Coatlicue). Toci was considered to be the mother of the gods, and the feast of Ochpaniztli (feast of sweeping) was dedicated to her. She was depicted with a broom in her hands, and we recall that Coatlicue was impregnated while the goddess was sweeping the hill of Coatepec.

According to Durán, Toci's feast was performed in the Templo Mayor. The most significant act in the feast was the sacrifice of a woman who was carried to the top of the temple back to back with a man and beheaded there. Afterward the man was dressed in the skin of the sacrificed woman and in the weaving she had done before her death. Some Huastecans accompanied her. Durán wrote:

> They dressed the Indian that way, bringing him before the public, led by those Huastecs and also his servants, all dressed for war. While they left by way of the chambers, all the leaders and nobles of the city were assembled and lined up there, very well armed with swords and shields . . . some of them descending from the top of

---

[69.] Sahagún 1956.
[70.] Sahagún 1956.

the temple and others coming from the outside. They feigned a skirmish and a combat that looked like the real thing.[71]

Afterward they sacrificed the captives in a manner significantly related to the myths. They tied them to logs and hurled them down before beheading them. Durán continued, "And they fell from the top of the logs and they crashed so hard below that they were torn apart."

One interesting aspect of this hill-temple relationship is the portrayal of the battles that were staged there during the feasts of deities associated with the myth.

3. The ritual of sacrifice. From written sources it is clear that the different types of sacrifice carried out in the Templo Mayor in some way recalled the relationship they had with the events in the myth. This fact, found in many religions, that a sacrifice represents a deity; the custom of throwing down the bodies and dismembering them; the beheading—all remind us of what Huitzilopochtli did to Coyolxauhqui. The sacrificed were generally war captives, just as the goddess was her brother's captive.

4. In the Códice Azcatitla is a very interesting representation of what we have been talking about. Coatepec is painted with four serpents emerging from it, and on the top we see a temple over which stands Huitzilopochtli, dressed as a hummingbird, with a spear in his right hand and in his left a shield or buckler. Between the hill with the serpents and the temple we see in Latin letters "Cohuatep." In front of those figures is another temple from which a serpent, bearing a kind of banner on its back, descends. Above the temple and the image can be read "Xiuhcohual oncatemoc." All of these images evidently refer to the myth of the battle at Coatepec. The glyph for the hill of the serpents is there, as is Huitzilopochtli in the act of combat above the representation of the temple. The other temple with the descending serpent is also quite clear. The Nahuatl text

---

[71.] Durán 1967.

refers to the descent of the fire serpent, which was Huitzilopochtli's weapon and was also represented during the feast of Panquetzaliztli as described previously.

5. In his "Descripción, historia y exposición del Códice Borbónico" of 1898, Francisco del Paso y Troncoso referred to the Templo Mayor as Coatepec. In describing one of the plates, the author said,

> Let us examine the painting by parts. To the right is the great temple of Uitcil-opoxtli, above which a slave woman is being sacrificed. Notice that of all the ones pictured in our pictorial manuscript, it is the highest and the largest. They called it Koatépetl, or "the hill of the snake," as I have said elsewhere, not only because that name commemorates the site where this principal god was born but because all those raised temples were considered to be hills.[72]

Regarding the Tlaloc side, Paso y Troncoso asked if one should consider all the temples of Tlaloc to be located on the tops of hills. For our part, we had already proposed that the Tlaloc side, like that of Huitzilopochtli, symbolized a hill: "In regard to the Tlaloc temple, it would not be strange to consider it a hill, like that of Huitzilopochtli, because some of the sacrifices in honor of the god of rain were performed on the tops of some hills, as in the months of Atlacahualo and Tozoztontli."[73] It not only represents a hill, as we see in the Códice Borbónico, but specifically Tonacatepetl, Mountain of Our Sustenance.[74]

The chronicles tell us that there were various festivals dedicated to the god of water or to deities related to fertility and corn. Among these festivities were the ones already mentioned, in which the god was worshiped in the lake, at his shrine in the Templo Mayor, and particularly at a hill called Mount Tlaloc.

[72.] Paso y Troncoso 1981. León Portilla (1978) also writes about the Hill of Coatepec. Also interesting is Zantwijk 1981.

[73.] Matos Moctezuma 1980.

[74.] Broda 1987.

Durán described the ritual of Huey Tozoztli: "All these games and festivites were carried out in an [artificial] forest set up in the courtyard of the temple in front of the image of the god Tlaloc. In the middle of the forest was planted a very large tree. It was the tallest that could be found in the woods, and it was called Tota, which means Our Father." Later he added, "Before the actual day of the feast of this god, a small forest was set up in the courtyard of the temple in front of the shrine of the idol Tlaloc. There many bushes, little hills, branches, and rocks were placed, all of which seemed the work of nature yet [were] not arranged in imitation of nature."[75]

Just as a boy was sacrificed inside a pavilion on the hill, they brought a girl to another pavilion and placed her in front of the idol. Then they took her with Tota to the drain of the lake and sacrificed her. The Templo was an intermediary place between the ceremony on Mount Tlaloc and the one on the lake.

Several other facts can be derived from what we have just discussed. If we look at the Templo Mayor from the front, we see that it was divided into two parts: the south side, devoted to war (Huitzilopochtli) and everything related to death, and the north side, devoted to Tlaloc and fertility, related to life. Here life and death acquire importance as contradictory but dialectically united elements. It is clear that death on Huitzilopochtli's side also implied life through sacrifice and, further, that the Templo possessed three elements necessary for life: earth (the terrestrial level of the Templo and of Coatlicue), water (Tlaloc), and the sun (Huitzilopochtli). The duality of life-death here acquired all its meaning, and the temple contained both aspects. Seen in this way, the temple could be said to show the faces of life and death. As an additional fact, we will mention that the four funerary urns found so far were on Huitzilopochtli's side, the side of war and death. Two of them date from stage II (approximately A.D. 1390) and two from stage IVb (A.D. 1470). Another important fact is that two of the places to which an individual would go

---

[75.] Durán 1971: 160.

after death were associated with the gods of the Templo Mayor: Tlalocan (Tlaloc) and the sun (Huitzilopochtli).

If we look at the temple from above, we could also see the four directions of the universe by drawing intersecting lines crosswise from corner to corner. The orientation of the Templo toward the west and the importance of Huitzilopochtli's struggle with the Huitznahua are evidently related to the sun's daily journey, in which it moved further to the south. This natural event, seen from the Templo Mayor, was expressed in the mythical fight.

And a final important aspect: according to Mexica cosmovision, the Templo Mayor as the fundamental center of all the cosmic order was the place where the gods coming from the different levels arrived on earth. Every cosmic event can be found in this structure, which was not a mere building but the place where the universal equilibrium of the Fifth Sun resided.

Phenomenon and Essence in the Templo Mayor

In Chapter 1 we pointed out that we used, among others, methodological concepts that distinguished between an investigation based on the phenomenological (that is, the external and empirical) and an investigation that focused on the interior of those phenomena to examine the essence that produced them. In this way *phenomenon* and *essence* played an important role in letting us go beyond just the data itself to determine to some extent the motives that led to particular phenomena and the relationships that existed among them. Looking at these not simply as cause and effect but rather as a dialectic relationship, we must ask a final question on the basis of all our new information. This question was also the first we asked: What underlies the symbolism of the Templo Mayor, and what are its full implications?

To answer that question, we begin with an analysis of Mexica society. From this we deduce that the survival of their society depended on two fundamental factors: agricultural production and war. Our initial question arose from that understanding, and we return to it with ampler and more detailed information. We believe that on this basis we can assert that the presence of Tlaloc and Huitzilopochtli in the Templo

Mayor and all it contained was closely linked to the fundamental needs of the economic bases that sustained the Mexica.

A quick survey of the contents of the offerings shows us something important. Tlaloc was represented in stone masks and figurines, ceramics, etc., mostly coming from areas under Mexica control (Guerrero and the Mixteca), as well as by elements intimately associated with the god, such as a great quantity and variety of biological remains, conch shells and shells, corals, fish, birds, turtles, etc., from both coasts. Symbols related to the god, such as canoes, serpents, and other things, were found as well. We can state, without a doubt, that the great majority of material found was associated in some way with Tlaloc. We also found a symbolic presence of Huitzilopochtli in knives, decapitated skulls, and especially in the great quantity of material that came from areas conquered in war.

All this material found in the Templo Mayor was systematically placed in different offerings following a predetermined plan. In other words, there is a *language* in the placing of the materials inside each offering that should be studied. Thus each object had a specific symbolism depending on its location in relation to the Templo and its placement inside the offering. Remember that most of the offerings were placed on particular axes. On the main facade there are three: at the juncture of the two staircases and at the middle of each one. The same axes are found on the rear of the Templo. In the middle of the north and the south facades, there are very rich offerings that are similar in their contents. The corners of the Templo are also important places.

A study of the contents of each offering and the association of the objects to one another has been done.[76] Most of them have their own orientation and center, relating them to the fundamental center of the Templo. This accounts for the possible presence of the old god of fire (Xiuhtecuhtli) in the shape of an elderly, toothless man who presides over many of the offerings. As you may recall, this god implies the concept of Ometeotl, who is found at the center, in the navel. In an offering excavated in the back side of the Templo Mayor on the edge of the ceremonial precinct, he was found in the exact center, with four large greenstone

---

[76.] [Translators' note] López Luján 1993, 1994.

beads at the ends of the cist. Those representations of resting gods must be studied in depth because they are extremely important in the context of the offerings and in their relationship to the Templo Mayor. At this time we believe that all of the material discovered very clearly reinforces the hypothesis we posed at the beginning: that agricultural production and everything related to it (fertility, water, land, etc.) and war, as a means to provide Tenochtitlan with necessary products from the conquered areas, were the main factors around which the phenomena described revolve, are produced and reproduced.

Our hypotheses,[77] conceived and presented in a very general way in the first phase of our project, after a study of the chronicles and archaeological information, led us to frame the problem to be investigated from those perspectives. With the new information obtained in our second phase, the excavation, we can now test our initial hypothesis, thus leading to our third phase, the interpretation of the material retrieved. This will either support our investigations, correct them, or even lead us to reconsider what we have said here. The process of investigation has not ended. To the contrary, new possibilities have opened that will lead to a fuller knowledge of the societies that preceded us.

[77.] Matos Moctezuma 1980.

Appendix 1

Photographs of the Templo Mayor

General view of the Templo Mayor.

Frog altar, stage IVb (A.D. 1470).

Clay funerary jar found next to Coyolxauhqui (39 cm high).

Stairway of stage III (A.D. 1431), with reclining sculptures.

Obsidian funerary urn found under the floor of stage II
(A.D. 1390).

Vase depicting death.

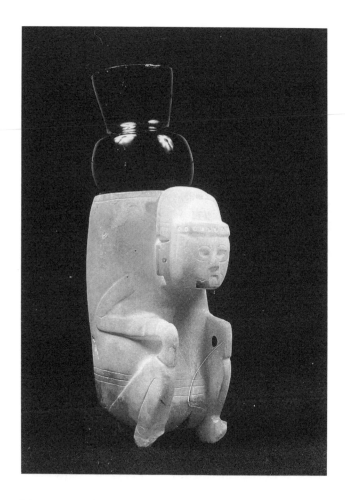

Alabaster urn found under the floor of stage II (A.D. 1390).

Clay funerary urn found near Coyolxauhqui under the
floor of stage IVb (A.D. 1470).

Sculpture of Tlaltecuhtli, the earth monster.

Detail of the balustrade with an eagle head leading to the Eagle Knights precinct (A.D. 1500).

Polychrome *chac-mool* found at the entrance to the Tlaloc shrine, stage II (A.D. 1390).

Clay jar with a representation of Tlaloc.

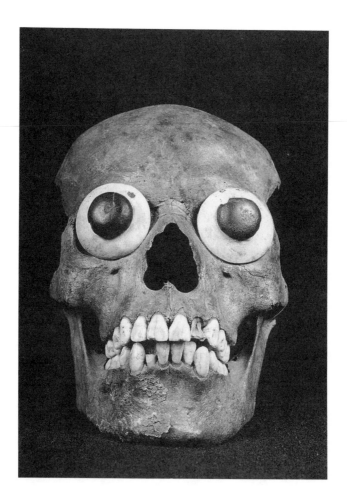

Skull with incrustations of shell and hematite.

Stone jar with a representation of Tlaloc.

Sculpture of Xiuhtecutli, the god of fire.

Stone sculpture of Huehueteotl, the old god.

Knife with face and base made of copal.

A stone marine conch, symbol of fertility.

Face carved in stone from stage II (A.D. 1390). Note the sacrificial stone behind it.

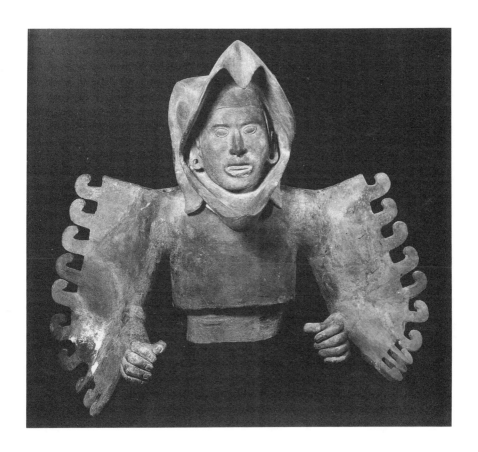

Detail of a clay Eagle Knight (A.D. 1500).

Principal facade of platform, stage IVb (A.D. 1470).

Tzompantli altar to the north of the Templo Mayor (A.D. 1500).

Appendix 2

Nahua Poems

Included here are twenty-five poems taken primarily from Angel María Garibay's work *Poesía náhuatl*, published in three volumes by the Universidad Nacional Autónoma de México (UNAM). They contain some important features related to what we have stressed throughout this book. On the one hand is constant anxiety, an uncertainty about death that the poets expressed through "flower and song," through poetry. On the other hand, they tell of the desire for death through combat or sacrifice, death by the obsidian edge, which would allow the warrior to accompany the sun. Ideology determined where the deceased would go and awarded the best destiny to the warriors, who were necessary for the survival of Tenochtitlan. It was their privilege to accompany the sun and, at the end of four years, to be converted into birds with beautiful feathers. Their transcendence was guaranteed . . .

1

    Emeralds,
turquoise,
are your chalk and your pen,
o you for whom all live!

    Now the princes
feel happy,
with flowery death by the obsidian edge,
with death in war.

2

1   Emeralds, gold
are your flowers, o God!

2   Only your riches,
o you for whom all live,
death by the obsidian edge,
death in war.

3   You will make yourself known
through death in war.

4   On the edge of war, near the conflagration,
you reveal yourself.

5   The shield dust is scattered,
the mist of darts is there.

6   Is this in truth
the place to reveal
the place of mystery?

7   Only the fame,
the title,
perishes in the war:
one is taken a little nearer
to the place of the fleshless.

6   Only with trembling flowers
         does one emerge . . . [end of text].

3
Warrior Chant

As much as I weep,
as much as I grieve,
as much as my heart cries out,
will I not have to go to the Realm of Mystery?
        On this earth our hearts say,
"Would that we were not mortal, o princes!
        Where is the region where there is no death?
May I not go there?
        Perchance does my mother live there in the Region of Mystery?
Perchance does my father live there in the Region of Mystery?"
        My heart trembles . . . I must not die . . .
I am filled with anguish!

                    *

        You left your fame assured on earth,
you, Prince Tlacahuepan:
Even now they offer to serve;
Even now men stand up
before him who makes the world live:
One comes to be born, one comes to live
on the earth!
        The banners interlace on the plain;
the obsidian flowers are mingled;
the chalk rains down, the feathers rain down:
I know that Tlacahuepan walks there.
        You came to see what your heart desired:
Death by the obsidian edge!

For a very brief time one is lent
the glory of him for whom all live.
One comes to be born, one comes to live
on earth!
With your golden skin, sprinkled with jade,
you are happy in the midst of the field of battle.
You came to see what your heart desired:
Death by the obsidian edge!

At last our death came to an end.
We of Zacatlan are famous.
Our fame is known there;
The Giver of Life is happy with us.
The god is worshiped
Before the Hill of the Shield.
The earth shakes, it gyrates in circles;
a rain of darts falls, the dust rises.
The god is worshiped
Before the Hill of the Shield.

4
Warrior Ardor

When the bells sound, the dust rises:
God, the Giver of Life, is delighted.
The shield flowers open their petals;
terror is spread, the earth trembles.
Here the flowers are gathered
in the midst of the plain.
The beginning is on the edge of the war,
in the midst of the plain.
The dust rises, making circles, with flowers of death,
o chiefs! o princes! o Chichimec!
Do not be cowardly, my heart:
There in the middle of the plain I seek death by the obsidian edge.
Our hearts desire only death in war.

So that there, close to the battle,
I desire death by the obsidian edge.
That is what my heart wants, the obsidian death.
    The clouds rise;
The Giver of Life becomes springtime;
with that the Eagle and the Jaguar are anointed.
The fire of the chiefs opens like a flower.
    Let us still enjoy,
still enjoy, o princes,
that in the midst of the plain one comes to live,
and there we borrow the shield flowers,
the ardor of battle.

5

1   As if they were flowers,
     songs are our garments, o friends.
     With them we come to live on earth.

2   Our song is real;
     our flowers are real,
     the beautiful song.
     Even though it be jade,
     even though it be gold,
     or broad quetzal feathers . . .
     May I make it here last by the drumbeat!
     Perhaps our death on earth may
     disappear?
     I am a singer.
     May it be so.

3   We rejoice with songs;
     we bedeck ourselves with flowers here.
     Do our hearts really understand?
     Must we abandon this when we depart?
     For this I weep, I become desolate!

4   Is it true that no one
will exhaust your riches,
your flowers, o Supreme Arbiter?
Must we abandon them when we leave?
For this I weep, I become desolate!

5   With flowers the nobility
here weave
their friendship.
Let us enjoy them,
their common home is the earth.

6   In the place of mystery
must it still be that way?
Not as here on earth,
where only the flowers
and the songs last?

7   Only here one time
are there honors from one to the other.
Who is known that way over there?
Is there true life there?

8   There is no sadness there;
Nothing is remembered there . . . alas!
Is it truly our home?
Do we also live there?

6

1   Let there be mutual friendship!
Let us know one another!
Only with these flowers
will song be lifted there.
We may have gone to his house,
but our words, our song
will live on earth.

2   We will go, leaving, on our departure,
our sadness, our song.
One knows oneself only through him;
through him is the song made real.
      We may have gone to his house,
      but our words, our song
      will live on earth!

3   My heart hears a song . . .
I begin to cry;
I become sad . . .
With flowers we have to leave
this earth.
      We only lend it, one to the other!
Oh, we have to go to his house!

4   Let me make necklaces
of different flowers;
Let them be in my hand,
let my garland of flowers be . . .
      We have to leave
this earth.
We only lend it, one to the other!
Oh, we have to go to his house!

5   As emeralds we gather
your beautiful songs,
o Giver of Life,
as if a gift of friendship.
May we accomplish them fully
here on earth!

6   I, the singer, am saddened by this;
for this I weep,
flowers are not taken
there to his house;
the songs are not taken . . . ,

but live here on earth!
Enjoy them,
o friends!

7   Our friends
Let no one become sad here!
Can this earth be no one's home?
No one will remain! . . .
    Now the quetzal feather is torn;
    Now the painting fades;
    there the flower withers . . .
    Everything that exists is taken to
    his house!

8   This is how we are:
A brief moment at your side,
next to you, Giver of Life.
Only once does one come
to make himself known on earth!
No one will remain! . . .
    Now the quetzal feather is torn;
    now the painting fades;
    there the flower withers . . .
    Everything that exists is taken
    to his house!

7

1   Let your heart open like a flower.
Let your heart lift upward . . .
You despise me, you are preparing my death.
Now I am going to his house;
I am going to disappear . . .
It may be that you weep for me;
That you, my friend, are saddened for me . . .
but . . . I am going, I am going to his house.

2   My heart says nothing else.
         I will never come again;
         Never again will I walk on earth . . .
         I am going, I am going to his house.

8

1   We torture ourselves.
         This is no longer the home of humans.
         There with the fleshless,
         there in his house . . .
              Only for a brief time
         does the earth intervene between here and there!

2   We humans live on
         borrowed earth . . .
         There with the fleshless,
         there is his house . . .
              Only for a brief time
         does the earth intervene between here and there!

9

1   Your flowers open their buds like jewels,
         surrounded by their emerald foliage.
         They are in our hands.
         Those precious, fragrant flowers;
         they are our apparel, o princes.
              They are only on loan to us
              here on earth.

2   Valiant and beautiful flowers
         go on intertwining!
         They are in our hands.
         Those precious, fragrant flowers;
         they are our apparel, o princes.
              They are only on loan to us
              here on earth.

3   I become sad;
I become deathly pale . . .
From his house where we are going,
oh, there will be no return;
no one will come back here!
One time and forever we will go
there to where we are destined!

4   If only the flowers and the songs
could be taken to his house!
Let me go adorned
with the golden frangipani,
with lovely aromatic flowers.
They are in our hands . . .
oh, there will be no return;
no one comes back here!
One time and forever we will go
there to where we are destined!

10

1   With black flowers streaked with gold
the beautiful song is entwined.
You, the singer, come with it to embellish
the people.
With varied flowers
you clothe the people.
Enjoy it, o princes.

2   Does one live like this now
and live this way in the place of mystery?
Is pleasure still possible there?
Oh, only here on earth, with flowers, does one make oneself known;
One expresses oneself with flowers,
o my friend!

3   Adorn yourself with your flowers,
flowers the color of the shining guacamaya,
brilliant as the sun; with frangipani
we adorn ourselves here on earth,
but only here.

4   It is only for a brief moment;
for only a short time do we have his flowers
on loan.
      Now they are taken to his house,
to the place of the fleshless, also his house;
and our anguish will not cease with that,
nor our sorrow.

11

1   Shake the flowers,
seek the songs
in your house, o you for whom all live,
Aztatohua (Owner of Herons).
      I say, "Enjoy yourselves here."

2   Perhaps with this you will break,
perhaps now you will understand,
o Chichimec princes.
Now the earth is behind us!
      I say, "Enjoy yourselves here."

3   There is a blast of trumpets;
There is a celebration in
springtime next to the drum.
      Only for a short time is anyone here;
He comes to live scattering flowers with his hands,
Tenocelotzin
comes twenty times wearing necklaces
Molocotlatzin and Chiyauhcohuatzin.
      One doesn't live two times.
Is the one that makes all live here on earth
lacking friends?

4   And he yearns for flowers
and lifts song,
just as the princes do.
The prince Cohuatzin
Tlacomihuatzin
is fanned with that
in the assembly of Eagles and Jaguars,
Xayacamachan,
       One doesn't live two times.
Is the one that makes all live here on earth
lacking friends?

12
Anguish Facing Death

I feel intoxicated, I weep, I suffer,
when I know, say, and remember:
       Oh, that I might never die!
       Oh, that I might never perish!
Where is there no death?
Where is there victory?
       That is where I would be . . .
       Oh, that I might never die!
       Oh, that I might never perish!

13
The Mystery of Death

What are you thinking about, upon what are you meditating,
o my friends?
       Do not meditate; beside us,
the beautiful flowers are being born!
Thus they delight the Giver of Life.
All of us meditate, all of us remember;
we become sad here on earth.
       It is the way all of the princes
are made—with sorrow and anguish.

Come here, my friend.
What are you thinking about; what do you ponder?
We are forever alone here on earth.
　　Don't be sad. I know sorrow.
We always live with anguish and sorrow here on earth.
　　Anger and bitterness came here from
the Giver of Life: We live within it.
Don't weep for the Eagles and the Jaguars.
All of us will disappear; no one will remain!
Think about it, Huexotzinca princes;
they could be gold,
they could be jade. All will go to the Realm of Mystery.
No one will remain.
　　I weep and still I lament,
when I remember the jades and the jewels
that you, o God, hid and enshrouded.
　　What will give solace to our hearts?
What will put an end to our sorrow?
　　I have only suffered, although your flowers are beautiful,
although your songs are lovely.
　　Is it possible for Ayocuatzin to return?
Will he be seen again?
Will it be possible to talk to him here beside the drums?

14
Elegy

As for me, I say,
　　"Alas, only for a brief instant!
Just as the magnolia opens its petals!
We have come here, friends, only to wither here
on this earth!
　　But now let bitterness cease;
Now give pleasure to your flesh.
　　But how do we eat? How do we give ourselves pleasure?
There our songs are born; there the kettledrum came to life.

I have suffered here on earth
where they lived.
Friendship will develop;
the community will grow next to the drums.
Will I, perhaps, still come?
Will I still sing a song?
But I am alone here. They are gone.
I have to abandon myself to forgetfulness and oblivion.
Let us believe our heart:
Is the earth our home?
We live in a place of sorrow and anguish.
For this only I sing and I ask,
"What flower will I plant another time?
What maize will I sow again?
Will my father and my mother produce new fruit,
fruit that will prosper on earth?"
This is the reason for my weeping.
No one is here; they have left us orphans on earth.
Where is the path
that leads to the Realm of the Dead,
where the fleshless are?
Is there life there in that region,
in which one, in some way, may exist?
Are our hearts still conscious?
Humans are hidden by the coffer and the box, and wrapped in cloth
by the Giver of Life.
Will I see them there?
Will I set my eyes on the faces
of my mother and father?
Will they still come to give me
their song and their word?
I am looking for them: No one is there.
They left us orphans here on earth.

15
Sorrow and Life

Although we are sad, let's enjoy the spring,
the Giver of Life makes us live in the midst of colors.
    He knows and he orders
how we humans will die.
No one, no one, no one, in truth, lives here!
    In vain I was born, in vain I came into the world.
I am suffering.
Oh, that I had never come into this world!
    I wish I had never been born!
And I say, "What will the surviving children do?
    Let me not offend anyone . . .
Should I be shy and keep my place?
    Is suffering my destiny?
O my friend, my heart cries out in anguish;
We live among afflictions on earth.
    How can we live with others?
If we live in vain we offend others!"
    One must live in peace, one must surrender
and walk with a bent-down head among others!
    Do not torture yourself, my heart.
Do not meditate on it any longer.
It is hard to live on a grieving earth.
And it is true that the sorrow will increase
[but] before you and at your side,
o Giver of Life!

16
Divine Glory and Human Misery

O Lord of the World, we give you pleasure here.
Next to you, no one feels desolate, o Giver of Life.
    You esteem us as if we were flowers;
here we your friends wither.

As if they were emeralds, you crush them:
like pictures in books, you erase them.
    Everyone that lives goes to the Kingdom of Death,
the place where all of us will be lost.
    How do you value us, o God?
As we live, so we perish
and as humans keep on dying!
Where are we going?
    I weep because of this.
When he who gives life is bored,
the jade is breaking, the feather rips.
You are mocking us; we are nothing,
and you value us as nothing.
You do away with us; you destroy us here!
    O Giver of Life, you give shelter and support
to your creatures.
No one says that they are desolate at your side
if they invoke you!
    Here at your side the emeralds flourish,
the fine feathers open. That is your heart,
o Giver of Life.
No one says that they are desolate at your side
if they invoke you!
    For a short time we live in happiness.
Enjoy it. For a brief time there is festivity.
In all of that time there is glory.
    No one is truly your friend.
For only a brief moment you lend us your flowers,
flowers that wither!
    When they bloom, it is you on your canopied throne,
in royal dignity in the midst of the plain,
command and dignity interwoven
with the flowers of war,
flowers that wither!

Nothing said here is true,
o you who give life.
Everything is like a dream, like what is said
when waking from a dream.
That is what we say on earth.
None of us speaks truth on earth!
    And even if handfuls of emeralds
were given to us, o Giver of Life,
not even when with jewels we beseeched you;
when we pleaded with you,
the nobility, the Eagle, the Jaguar,
none of us speaks truth on earth!
    O Giver of Life who mocks us;
it is only a dream we pursue, friends.
Our hearts are confident,
but the Giver of Life mocks us!

17
Ayocuan's Poem

Now let us enjoy ourselves, o my friends;
let the embracing begin here.
Here we live on a flowery land;
here no one can put an end to the flowers and the song
that have their mansion in the house of the Giver of Life.
    Only for a short time on earth:
It will not be the same in the Realm of Mystery.
Is there perhaps enjoyment there, is there friendship?
No, only here. We have come to know each other on earth.

18
An Anonymous Poet

Let my heart resolve
to wish only for the shield of flowers.
They are the flowers of god.

What will my heart do?
Do we come here, pass through earth in vain?
 I, too, will disappear
like the flowers that have perished.
Will my fame be nothing one day?
Will nothing of my name be left here on earth?
At least flowers, at least songs . . .
 What will my heart do?
Do we come here, pass through earth in vain?

19
A Poet's Anguish

My heart aches, o my friends,
when I say
my heart has wandered on earth.
I have been asking it how we live,
a place of pleasure, of well-being, and of happiness
with others.
I have not yet been taken to the Realm of Mystery!
 My heart knows it well,
truly I say, my friends.
Everyone who prays to god
injures his heart in doing it.
Is there nothing else on earth?
Isn't it possible to be born two times?
 Is it true one lives in the Realm of Mystery,
in the sky?
 One is happy only here.

20
Uncertainty About the End

Where will I go, alas?
Where will I go?
 Where is the Duality?
It is difficult, so difficult!

Is everyone's home there,
where the fleshless are,
in the sky?
Or perhaps here on earth is where
the fleshless dwell!
    We go completely, we go completely.
No one remains on earth!
    Who is left to say, "Where are our friends?"
Be happy!

21
Fleeting Life

I begin the song; I want to take
your flowers, Giver of Life.
We play on the flowered drums.
This is our duty here on earth.
    Flowers that cannot be taken;
songs that cannot be taken to the Realm of Mystery!
We vanish entirely. No one remains on earth.
One day at least, o my friends,
we will have to leave our flowers, our songs.
We have to leave the eternal earth.
    Let us rejoice, friends, let us rejoice.

22
The Enigma of Living

I weep, I am aggrieved when I remember
that we will leave the beautiful flowers, the lovely songs.
    Now let us rejoice, let us sing.
We all will go and disappear in his house!
    Which one of you, friends, doesn't know it?
My heart mourns, is filled with anger.
One is not born two times, not twice is one a human:
only once does one walk on earth.

If even for a short time
I could be at their side . . .
It will not be. I will never have pleasure, never enjoy!
    Where is the place for my heart to live?
Where is my house? Where is my enduring home?
    Here on earth I only suffer.
    Do you suffer, my heart?
Do not grieve on this earth;
it is my destiny; know it well!
    How did I deserve life;
how did I deserve to be a human?
He did it!
    There where there is no life
things are set swirling.
That is what my heart says.
And god, what does he say?
We don't truly live here.
We have not come to last on earth.
    Oh, I must leave the beautiful song, the lovely flower,
and seek the Realm of Mystery.
    Soon he will be bored.
The beautiful song is only lent to us.

23
Vanity of the Song

Even in vain, my friends, delight
in our song, in our song.
    You take your precious drum;
you scatter and spread flowers.
They wither!
    Here also we sing our new songs,
and we have new flowers in our hands.
    Delight in them, friends.
Let our bitterness and our sadness perish with them!
    Let no one be sad, let no one remember the earth.
Our flowers and our beautiful songs are here!

Delight in them, friends.
Let our bitterness and our sadness perish with them!
    Only here on earth, o friends,
are we lent to each other.
    We must leave the beautiful songs.
We must leave the beautiful flowers.
    This is why I am sad: for your song, Giver of Life . . .
We must leave the beautiful songs.
We must leave the beautiful flowers.

24
Songs of Anguish

I gladden your heart, o Giver of Life:
I offer you flowers; I lift songs to you.
    That I may give you pleasure even for a short time,
you will tire of it some day.
    When you destroy me,
when I must die.
    Must your heart recoil, o Giver of Life?
I offer you flowers; I lift songs to you.
    That I may give you pleasure even for a short time,
you will tire of it some day.
    When you destroy me,
when I must die.

*

You disperse what is orderly.
You do not gather what is dispersed, o Giver of Life,
the one who lives and rejoices, the one who lives happy on this earth.
    This is why I weep, this is why I am afflicted.
    That is what my heart says, that is all it considers:
You are not happy, you have no joy.
    This is why I weep, this is why I am afflicted.

*

Is the word of god fulfilled on earth?
Can one live there? Are we unfortunate?
You torment us.
    Suffer, there is nothing else!
    Wherever it is sought,
wherever it is invoked, wherever acclaimed,
his word is sought.
Can one live there? Are we unfortunate?
You torment us.
    Suffer, there is nothing else!

*

    What do you want, o Giver of Life?
Will I be unhappy one day, beside you?
And yet will I still suffer?
    And even when my time comes, when my death occurs,
there will be springtime flowers;
and even when my time comes, fragrant flowers will bloom,
the golden flowers with a thousand petals . . . !

*

    The perfumed flower of Tamoanchan,
I lift up the red flower in Tamoanchan.
    It is the book of your heart:
It is your song, o God.
    You know well how it is raised and how humans are
told, painted and warned with it here.
    Your heart is your song and your book.
    Our sadness is entwined with something precious:
it is your song, o God.

*

    Are we going to let pleasure be destroyed
after we are gone?
Will joy be the friend of our flowers?

Let us enjoy ourselves now!
Our hearts are happy now;
O friends, we must leave.
Let us enjoy ourselves now!

*

Who knows this?
Now, tomorrow, or the day after we must go;
And even if this happens, we must remember:
Is it really true we come here to live?
You of the Near and Nigh,
you are our friend:
and you will tire of having pleasure,
you will be bored on earth,
where we lift our song to you.
Don't we know it in our hearts?
The Giver of Life will tire, will feel bored,
and he will destroy us.
Don't we know it in our hearts?
We have come only to make songs on the earth
and to know each other at the place of the drums.
You are our friend,
nothing will succeed,
nothing will perish on the earth!

25
The Warriors' Song

Lift up the kettledrum, princes!
In spite of everything, enjoy yourselves here before the god.
Weeping takes place, tears flow,
here, before god, in the place of the kettledrums.
Prince Motecuzoma swings like an eagle,
circles like a jaguar when he adorns his men.
Go test yourselves on the field of battle!
King Motecuzoma comforts the different Eagles,

the different Jaguars, and the different princes
when he adorns his men.
Go test yourselves on the field of battle!

He strengthens the hearts of men
with the chalk and feather flowers.
He enraptured men's hearts
with the Eagle flower.
That is why they went, they went.
those Chichimec princes:
King Motecuzoma, Chahuacueye, Cueyatzin
resembled the hummingbird.
Truthfully now, you have not seen Xaltemoctzin,
you were not tested by King Quinantzin,
Tzihuacpopocatzin.
Soon the shield flower will slacken
and wither. You have only borrowed it,
o princes.
No one will see it wither
because we have to go to the Realm of Mystery.
We must step aside and leave our place
to others on this earth. You have only borrowed it,
o princes.
Now for this weep, o Chimalpopoca,
and you, Acolmitzin, and you, Tizahuactzin.
Lift up the kettledrum;
entertain the people, and drive off our sadness.
Where is the singer?
beat our kettledrum strongly;
entertain the people and drive off our sadness.

Like a white water lily of wind, the shield whirls,
like smoke the dust rises, whistle calls sound
here in Mexico Tenochtitlan.

It is the house of the shield, the house of combat.
Here is the Order of the Eagles;
It is the mansion of the Order of the Jaguars.
Here war rules; they whistle for battle.
Here are the flowers of Chimalpopoca.
It is not true, not reality, not a fact,
that all must stop, all must be extinguished.
Weep for that, o Chichimec,
You, Tlaixtoctin, weep for that.
The beautiful flowers of the Giver of Life are delightful.
Because you torment them, the hearts
of the princes are full of sorrow. What is left for them to do?
Resigned, we suffer;
Let us die thus. What could have been!
Let our friends speak to us;
Let the Eagles and the Jaguars reprimand us:
What can be done? Do it.
What can be done? Take it.
It is the flower of the Giver of Life.
They take it; it is taken in the place of anguish,
where glory is, next to glory,
on the battlefield.

Bibliography

CISINAH   Centro de Investigaciones Superiores del INAH
FCE   Fondo de Cultura Económica
INAH   Instituto Nacional de Antropología e Historia
INI   Instituto Nacional Indigenista
IPGH   Instituto Panamericano de Geografía e Historia
SEP   Secretaría de Educación Pública
UNAM   Universidad Nacional Autónoma de México

Bate, F. 1984. "Hipótesis sobre la sociedad clasista inicial." *Boletín de Antropología Americana* 9.

Bierhorst, J. 1992. *History and Mythology of the Aztecs: The Codex Chimalpopoca.* Tucson: Univ. of Arizona Press.

Broda, J. 1987. "The Provenience of the Offerings: Tribute and *Cosmovision.*" In E. H. Boone, ed., *The Aztec Templo Mayor,* 211–256. Washington, D.C.: Dumbarton Oaks.

Caso, A. 1958. *The Aztecs: People of the Sun.* Norman: Univ. of Oklahoma Press.

Chavero, A. 1887. *México a través de los siglos.* 5 vols. Mexico: Ballesca.

Childe, G. 1961. *Man Makes Himself.* New York: New American Library.

Códice Chimalpopoca. 1945. Trans. F. P. Velázquez. Mexico: UNAM.

Dante, A. 1970. *The Divine Comedy.* Trans. C. Singleton. Princeton: Princeton Univ. Press.

Durán, D. de. 1967. *Historia de las Indias de la Nueva España e Islas de la Tierra Firme.* A. M. Garibay, ed. Mexico: Porrúa.

———. 1971. *Book of the Gods and Rites and the Ancient Calendar.* Trans. F. Horcasitas and D. Heyden. Norman: Univ. of Oklahoma Press.

Eliade, M. 1958. *Patterns in Comparative Religion.* New York: Sheed and Ward.

García Cook, A., and R. M. Arana. 1978. *Rescate arqueológico del monolito Coyolxauhqui.* Mexico: INAH.

Garibay, A. M. 1964–1968. *Poesía náhuatl.* 3 vols. Mexico: UNAM.

González Torres, Y. 1958. "El dios Huitzilopochtli en la peregrinación mexica." *Anales del INAH* 19: 179–190.

———. 1975. *El culto a los astros entre los mexica.* Setentas 217. Mexico: SEP.

Heyden, D. 1981. "Caves, Gods, and Myths: World-view and Planning in Tenochtitlan." In E. P. Benson, ed., *Mesoamerican Sites and World-views,* 1–40. Washington, D.C.: Dumbarton Oaks.

"Historia de los mexicanos por sus pinturas." 1941 [1855–1866]. In J. García Icazbalceta, ed., *Nueva colección de documentos para la historia de México.* Mexico: Chavez Hayhoe.

Humboldt, A. 1891. *Sitios de las Cordilleras.* Madrid: Gaspar Editores.

Jensen, A. E. 1963. *Myth and Cult Among Primitive Peoples.* Chicago: Univ. of Chicago Press.

Kirchhoff, P. 1943. "Mesoamerica." *Acta Americana* 1: 92–107.

Kirchhoff, P., L. O. Güemes, and L. Reyes García, eds. 1976. *Historia Tolteca-Chichimeca.* Mexico: INAH/CISINAH.

León Portilla, M. 1963. *Aztec Thought and Culture.* Norman: Univ.of Oklahoma Press.

————. 1978. *El Templo Mayor de Tenochtitlan: su espacio y tiempo sagrados.* Mexico: INAH.

Lévi-Strauss, C. 1963. *Structural Anthropology.* Harmondsworth: Penguin Books.

López Austin, A. 1988. *Human Body and Ideology.* Trans. T. Ortiz de Montellano and B. R. Ortiz de Montellano. Salt Lake City: Univ. of Utah Press.

López Luján, L. 1993. *Las ofrendas del Templo Mayor de Tenochtitlan.* Mexico: INAH.

————. 1994. *The Offerings of the Templo Mayor of Tenochtitlan.* Trans. B. R. Ortiz de Montellano and T. Ortiz de Montellano. Boulder: Univ. Press of Colorado.

Marx, K. 1970. *A Contribution to a Critique of Political Economy.* New York: International Publishers.

Matos Moctezuma, E. 1978a. "Internacionalismo, nacionalismo, indigenismo y explotación." In *Treinta años después.* Mexico: INAH.

————. 1978b. "El Projecto Templo Mayor." *Boletín del INAH* 24.

————. 1978c. *Muerte al filo de obsidiana.* Mexico: INAH.

————, ed. 1979. *Excavaciones arqueológicas en el centro de la ciudad de México.* Mexico: INAH.

————. 1980. "El Templo Mayor de Tenochtitlan: economía e ideología," *Boletín de Antropología Americana* 1.

————. 1981. *Una visita al Templo Mayor.* Mexico: INAH.

————. 1982a. "El proceso de desarroyo en Mesoamérica." In *Teorías, métodos y técnicas en arqueología.* Mexico: IPGH.

————, ed. 1982b. *El Templo Mayor: excavaciones y estudios.* Mexico: INAH.

Matos Moctezuma, E., and V. Rangel. 1982. *El Templo Mayor de Tenochtitlan, planos, cortes y perspectivas.* Mexico: INAH.

Mauss, M., and H. Hubert. 1970. *Lo sagrado y lo profano.* Barcelona: Barral.

Nowotny, K. 1961. *Tlacuilolli*. Berlin: Gebr. Mann.

Paso y Troncoso, F. 1981 [1898]. "Descripción, historia y exposición del Códice Borbónico." In *Códice Borbónico*. Mexico: Siglo XXI Editores.

Sahagún, B. de. 1950–1970. *Florentine Codex*. Trans. A.J.O. Anderson and C. E. Dibble. Salt Lake City: Univ. of Utah Press.

———. 1956. *Historia de las cosas de la Nueva España*. 4 vols. Mexico: Porrúa.

Seler, E. 1963 [1905]. *Comentarios al Códice Borgia*. Mexico: FCE.

Tezozomoc, F. 1975. *Cronica Mexicayotl*. Mexico: UNAM.

Zantwijk, R. van. 1981. "The Great Temple of Tenochtitlan: Model of Aztec Cosmovision." In E. P. Benson, ed., *Mesoamerican Sites and World-views,* 71–86. Washington, D.C.: Dumbarton Oaks.

Index